Praise for The Stakes

"Shibley Telhami has become a voice of reason on American policy toward the Middle East. Few command such balanced knowledge and understanding, not only of Arabs and Israelis. Dr. Telhami's book presents an intriguing analysis of American stakes in the Middle East and a thoughtful argument for the compassionate and measured use of force."

—Jimmy Carter

"Shibley Telhami is the wisest commentator on Middle East affairs I know. In his latest book, *The Stakes*, he has outdone himself. Give this book to all your friends!"

—Samuel Lewis, Ambassador to Israel
(1977–1985, under Carter and Reagan)

"An important contribution to the much-needed American debate on where we go from here in the Middle East."

—L. Carl Brown, Foreign Affairs

"With this timely book, Americans now have a guide through the complex issues that confront our country in the Middle East. As we confront Iraq and try to advance Israeli-Palestinian peace, this book is particularly timely."

—William B. Quandt, University of Virginia

"A book of searing insights, based on thorough knowledge of the Middle East. Succinct and clearly written, objective and even-handed, everyone concerned with terror, conflict, and America's role in the region should read this book."

—Kenneth Waltz, Columbia University

"This book should be immediately read and pondered by top-level administration officials, their advisors, public opinion leaders, and all concerned citizens."

—Alexander L. George, Stanford University

"Shibley Telhami is one of the wisest commentators on the current problems in the Middle East. I highly recommend this fine book for all of its wisdom and balance."

—Rev. Theodore M. Hesburgh, C.S.C.,
president emeritus, University of Notre Dame

THE STAKES

AMERICA IN
THE MIDDLE EAST

*The Consequences of Power
and the Choice for Peace*

Shibley Telhami

Westview
PRESS

A Member of the Perseus Books Group

We acknowledge the organizations maintaining the following websites for use of their maps:

The Middle East: www.lib.utexas.edu/maps/middle_east_and_asia/ middleeast_ref01.pdf
The Arab World (with border added): www.aaiusa.org/images/arab_world_map.JPG and the U. S. Central Intelligence Agency
The Muslim World: www.lib.utexas.edu/maps/world_maps/muslim_distribution.jpg
Israel and the Palestinian Territories: www.lib.utexas.edu/maps/ middle_east_and_asia/middleeast_ref01.pdf

Westview Press books are available at special discounts for bulk purchases in the United States by corporations, institutions, and other organizations. For more information, please contact the Special Markets Department at the Perseus Books Group, 11 Cambridge Center, Cambridge MA 02142, or call (617) 252-5298.

Published in 2002 in the United States of America by Westview Press, 5500 Central Avenue, Boulder, Colorado 80301-2877, and in the United Kingdom by Westview Press, 12 Hid's Copse Road, Cumnor Hill, Oxford OX2 9JJ

First paperback printing, January 2004

Find us on the World Wide Web at www.westviewpress.com

A Cataloging-in-Publication data record for this book is available from the Library of Congress.

ISBN 0-8133-4291-0
University of Maryland First-Year Book 2004-2005

Set in 11.5-point New Caledonia by the Perseus Books Group

The paper used in this publication meets the requirements of the American National Standard for Permanence of Paper for Printed Library Materials Z39.48-1984.

10   9   8   7   6   5   4   3   2

To Kathryn Hopps, my partner and friend, my first point of reference, a source of unending inspiration and support, my wife.

CONTENTS

The Middle East

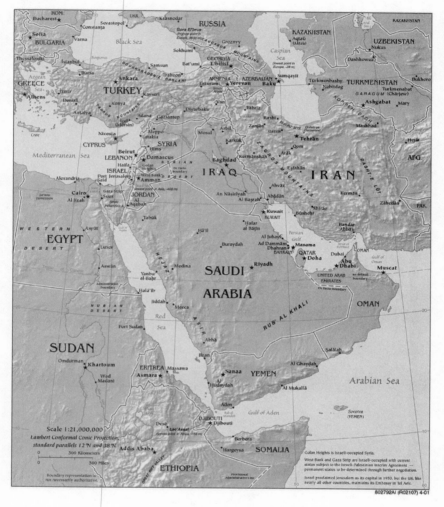

The Arab World

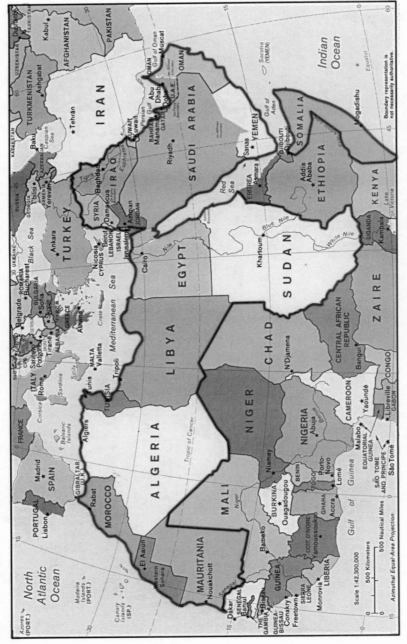

The Muslim World

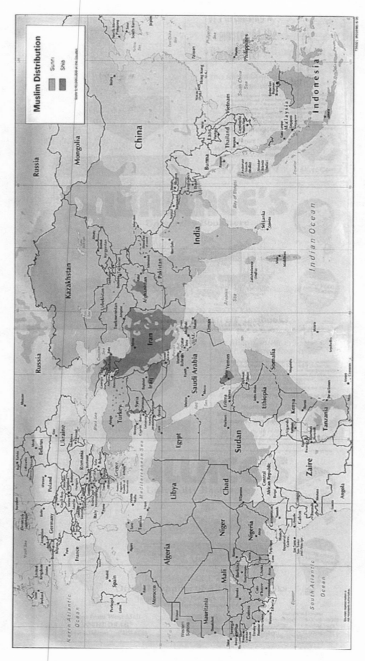

Muslim Distribution

- Sunni
- Shia

Israel and the Palestinian Territories

Base 802833 (A00853) 9-01

PREFACE

Heart-wrenching tragedies and crises test both individuals and groups. The horror that befell the United States on September 11, 2001, presented a serious challenge to every American, especially those who deeply care about peace in the Middle East. It wasn't simply the fear and sense of vulnerability, or astonishment at the degree of ruthlessness that the terrorists exhibited; even more, it was about profound questions that everyone asked—about who we are, what kind of world we live in, and who we want to be. We all understood that the choices we made in responding to this horror not only would affect the degree of future threat but also would define who we will become.

The attack was also a reminder of the danger of keeping quiet in the face of bloodshed, and of the need for everyone to keep a moral compass so as not to allow passions of the moment to dictate our actions. I understand the importance of power and the need to deploy it to counter threats. But I also believe in the prudent exercise of power, and in the limitation of power. Ultimately, I am a realist: Powerful actors can get away with a lot, including some imprudence. But in the end no one is powerful enough to overcome too much imprudence, and power is ultimately balanced by the degree to which its exercise motivates adversaries to act. At the same time, where there is an abundance of power, it should be pursued as an instrument of values; if the powerful cannot afford to act morally, who can?

The tragedy of 9/11 was painful for all Americans, especially those close to the scenes of death and destruction in New York, Washington, and Pennsylvania. Even before I could recover from the shock, I was called upon to put on my analyst hat, to appear in the media, to write. As I drove to the public broadcasting television station in Virginia to appear on the *NewsHour with Jim Lehrer*, I passed by the Pentagon, which was still on fire.

As I began writing in reaction to the attacks, I often felt tearful. I had two fears at once. The first was the obvious one: The threat of terrorism in the era of globalization made us literally fear for our children. The second fear was more subtle but equally haunting: What will these atrocities make of us? For these reasons, my first reaction (published in *The New York Times* on September 19, 2001) was about the "ends and means" of political action. I feared that the depth of our pain might incline us, the most powerful nation on earth, to forget that we cannot defend what we stand for by subverting our own values in the process of reacting to such attacks.

In the year that followed I wrote more than three dozen articles, gave dozens of lectures, and made many television and radio appearances to analyze the consequences of the attacks and try to understand how they had happened. These writings appeared in many newspapers: *The New York Times*, *The Washington Post*, the *Los Angeles Times*, *The Baltimore Sun*, *The Boston Globe*, the *San Jose Mercury News*, *Al-Hayat* (Arabic), *The Brookings Review*, *Current History*, and *The Middle East Journal*, among others. The response I received from people around the country was moving and heartening. One writer put it this way: "I wanted to tell you how grateful I am to you for what you said. . . . You know, when you get hit and they tell you it's your fault and you somehow deserved it, it creates a lot of resentment and it polarizes people horribly. After I heard you, though, I have felt a new sense of closeness—one voice sometimes is enough to change everything."

This writer, and many like her, helped sustain my uninterrupted efforts in the months that followed.

This book builds on these writings and reflections, and much that I have learned from others in the process, to put forth ideas about the issues that have preoccupied America and much of the world since 9/11 and are likely to affect U.S. foreign policy in the next decade. What is the nature of the terrorist threat? What is the role of Islam in Middle East terrorism? "Why do they hate us so much?" What is the role of public opinion in the Middle East? What is the role of the Arab-Israeli conflict? Is the Persian Gulf still important for the United States? What's in store for America's relations with Iraq? What are the stakes for our nation?

The book is primarily about the Arab world and U.S. relations with it, including in the Persian Gulf, and about the Arab-Israeli conflict. In it I often speak of "Arabs and Muslims" and the "Arab and Muslim worlds." In these cases, I examine the attitudes that are common in Muslim countries, including states that are Muslim but not Arab. Fifty-five states are members of the Organization of the Islamic Conference, and twenty-two states are members of the Arab League. Muslim Arabs constitute about a quarter of the world's 1.2 billion Muslims, and a minority of Arabs are not Muslim, including some Christians. Arab states are spread across North Africa and the Middle East. Many attitudes are commonly held by the public in both Arab and Muslim countries, especially on foreign policy, with important differences across Islamic countries and across Arab countries. However, in attitudes toward U.S. policy, the similarities are greater than the differences.

I am grateful to many people whose help has been essential. Some were collaborators with whom I have coauthored articles: Edward P. Djerejian, Fiona Hill, Steven Kull, and David Wippman. Barry Preisler and Michael Hopps provided very helpful comments and much support. Amy Pate and Ghada al-Madbouh helped with research. The Gallup Organization and Zogby International were very helpful in providing data. Westview Press editor Karl Yambert made excellent suggestions and kept me on track, and Holly Hodder provided constant encouragement. Others at Westview were also very helpful: Patricia Goodrich, Barbara Greer, and Greg Houle, and copyeditor Connie Oehring. My assistant, Aysha Ismail, who has been there throughout the trying months, provided even more support for this project. In addition, there were dozens of people from whom I benefited greatly in the many forums and debates that have taken place in the past year.

No one, however, contributed more than Kathryn Hopps, my intellectual companion, my friend and partner, my wife. Not only has she carried many of our mutual duties alone, including much of the care of our children, but she was also my first point of reference and my first editor and critic. I cannot forget the understanding and patience displayed by my nine-year-old daughter, Ruya, and my six-and-a-half-year-old son, Ramsey, throughout their summer vacation as I worked on this book. Nor can I forget the good manners of our summer guest, Ji-Yun Oh, who, at age nine, braved a trip alone from South Korea to spend time with Ruya.

Shibley Telhami

1

Understanding the Terrorist Threat

Shortly after the horror that befell America on September 11, 2001, I was invited to have lunch with a prominent congressional leader. The aim was to discuss the nature of the threat our nation faced and to explore the consequences of what had transpired for America's relations with the Middle East. My host was thoughtful, serious, and contemplative, but his mood was summarized by something he said at the outset of our meeting: "We are a powerful nation, but this type of terrorism could defeat us." Within weeks, however, following the collapse of the Taliban regime in Afghanistan, the reversal of the congressional mood was striking. It was a true reflection of America's emotional journey.

Indeed, the shift in America's mood in the months following that horrific day in September was breathtaking in its scope and unprecedented in its speed. From the strongest sense of vulnerability in recent history to the most strident self-confidence in memory after the seemingly easy success in toppling the Taliban regime in Afghanistan, the journey took but a few months.

At some level this rapid journey was healing to a nation whose confidence had been painfully shaken. At another level it was troubling. Certainly America has experienced many radical swings in its foreign policy in the past. But from the isolationism that followed World War I—carried out to a disastrous extreme, as witnessed in Pearl Harbor—to the ensuing interventionism that ended with the quagmire in Vietnam, the swings were almost generational. Rarely have such extreme shifts in mood been more rapid than in the autumn of 2001—and, perhaps, rarely as consequential.

Neither extreme is justified by reality. The United States remains the most powerful nation in the world today, but it is not powerful enough to confront the new global challenges alone or to justify the overconfidence that followed the toppling of the Taliban regime in Afghanistan. The rapidity of these mood shifts can in part be explained by the absence of a competing superpower and by the general speed of today's world. The information revolution carried the horror to every home worldwide within hours. The technological revolution enabled a remarkable military success with minimal American casualties thousands of miles from U.S. shores.

But these very factors that have led to bolstering a unilateralist trend in America's foreign policy have also raised global concerns about America's role in the world. There has been an equally dramatic shift in the global mood from empathy with America's pain and a sense of global vulnerability immediately after the attacks on the United States in September 2001 to a widening gap between America and other states. Resentment of U.S. power has grown in much of the world, and certainly in the Middle East.

Understandably, much of the American focus has been on the attitudes of the Middle East and Muslim countries, especially on the question many Americans have instinctively asked: "Why do they hate us so much?" But before addressing this question, and whether it is indeed true at all that "they hate us so much," we must put the Middle East in a global perspective. Although there are some unique aspects in the Middle Eastern view of the United States, it is also important to understand that much of the reaction of Arabs and Muslims to America's war on terrorism, and to American foreign policy more broadly, has not been significantly different from the reaction of people in other regions of the world.

It is not helpful to assume that the global reaction to America's mood in its declared war on terrorism is mere whining. And it is even more dangerous to assume that the global sentiment is inconsequential in light of America's significant powerful resources. Aside from the increased motivation for other states to coalesce in order to challenge America's power if America is seen to be embarking on a unilateralist course, the nature of the threat revealed by the horror of 9/11 cannot be addressed through coercive power alone. This issue is at the heart of the conflict of views between the United States and many other states in defining the terrorist threat that the world faces today. Indeed, the evolution of the degree of empathy with the United States in the months following September 2001 has been in large part a function of the evolving American view of the war on terrorism.

Conflicting Views of Terrorism

There are five significant differences between the views put forth by the United States and those of much of the world. In the rest of this chapter, I will highlight these key differences that explain the conflict between the United States and others over the most effective means to address terrorist threats.

1. Much of the world empathized with America's pain and supported its right of self-defense in light of the horrific attacks but did not see that right as enabling America to unilaterally define global terrorism beyond the immediate threat to its own soil.

2. The United States focused its effort in fighting terrorism on confronting the "supply side" of terrorism without equally addressing the "demand side," which many around the world see as critical.

3. The Bush administration defined terrorism as if it were an ideology, a political coalition, when in fact most

around the world understand it to be an immoral means employed by diverse groups for different ends.

4. In the U.S. view the central terrorist threat resides in "terrorist states," and some U.S. officials talk as if confronting those states could result in the defeat of the terror phenomenon. However, most around the world view terrorism as the antistate, as an increasingly threatening phenomenon in part because of the relative weakening of the state in an era of globalization.

5. The public discourse in America has associated terrorism in the Middle East, especially the suicide bombings, with aspects of the Islamic religion, even as President Bush has been careful to reject this notion, whereas many around the world see both the motives and the means of Middle Eastern terrorism to be less about Islam than about politics.

1. The Two Separate Missions

In the weeks following the events of 9/11, expressions of empathy with the United States pervaded the international community, including the Middle East. Even countries with whom the United States has had tense and often confrontational relationships, such as Iran, which remains on the State Department's list of "terrorist states," expressed unusual sympathy with America's pain. Iranian President Mohammad Khatami immediately issued a condemnation of "the terrorist attacks" and expressed "deep sorrow and sympathy" for the victims. Syria's young President Bashar Assad sent a letter of condolence to President Bush strongly condemning the terror attacks. In general, most leaders and governments recognized that the United States had a right to respond to the terror on its soil once the culprits were identified. But it is important to understand the sources of the early global support for America and why much of this support turned to resentment as the United States moved to define and wage its global war on terrorism.

Undoubtedly much of the sympathetic reaction was genuine, even as some harbored a wicked sense of satisfaction that America was now tasting what many around the world have suffered for too long. The magnitude of the human tragedy was inescapable given that the horror was transmitted almost live on television screens in much of the world. But the response was more than mere humanitarian reflex. America's vulnerability was in some ways the world's vulnerability. If such horror could befall the sole remaining superpower, then no one is immune. If the anchor of the international system is shaken, so is the entire global system. Even in the Middle East, where many already resented America and in some instances found pleasure in its pain, other voices saw the threat to the United States as a threat to them as well, not merely because America was seen as the anchor of the global system but also because it represented a dream to which many aspired. Though U.S. policy continued to receive criticism on the pages of newspapers in the Middle

East, a columnist of the influential Arabic daily *Al-Hayat*, for example, expressed his emotions this way on September 19, 2001: "The destruction of America is the destruction of the human dream across the world." In the Middle East, as in much of the world, there was, at least for a moment, a widespread sense eloquently expressed by one Frenchwoman that "today, we are all American."

Above all, it was clear that most governments around the world recognized America's right to respond with force. No state, let alone a superpower, could allow an attack of this magnitude to remain unanswered. No one could deny America's fundamental right of self-defense, regardless of how they viewed or defined terrorism.

This is not to say that most around the world felt that America should have a free hand in waging a global war on terrorism. Indeed, much of the early public reaction in the Middle East, as the United States geared up for its war on the Taliban regime in Afghanistan, was predicated on the assumption that the United States had presented insufficient evidence to prove responsibility, even though the Taliban regime had been highly unpopular in the broader Arab and Muslim worlds. Though many *governments* in the Middle East supported the U.S. campaign, their *publics* remained unpersuaded. (This regional public mistrust of the substantial evidence that the United States presented needs an explanation—it will be addressed in the next chapter.)

In the end, despite *public* distrust of America's intentions, at least in the Middle East, America's right to respond to the horror was strong enough to attract significant support from *states* for the campaign to overturn the Taliban regime and destroy Usama bin Laden's al-Qaeda. Even such states as Iran offered support for these operations, together with dozens of nations across the globe, especially in the Middle East, which participated in intelligence gathering, financial coordination, or providing help for the actual conduct of operations. Certainly, part of this governmental support was provided to avoid being targeted by a wounded and angry America. But few governments around the world seriously challenged the legitimacy of the first mission of responding to the attack by destroying al-Qaeda.

The White House defined another mission as an integral part of the global war on terrorism. In principle, this mission too received universal support, as shown by the passing of UN Security Council Resolution 1373 on September 28, 2001, obligating states to fight terrorism. But such a resolution was possible only because member states did not have to tackle the issue of defining terrorism. One thing was clear: Many states among those voting for the resolution did not see eye to eye with the United States on such a definition. Many feared that "terrorism" would become a convenient shorthand for the United States and other nations to label their enemies.

The United States commanded international moral authority after the September attacks to begin to find common ground in defining terrorism, even though there was no agreement about how to identify "terrorist groups." The administration needed to decide which of the thousands of terrorist groups around the world it would define as enemies.

President Bush refined this second mission by concentrating on terrorist groups with "global reach." But a central issue remained: which organizations to target. States differ widely on what they consider a "terrorist" group. Some governments classify mere opposition groups as terrorist. Others have refused to accept the U.S. classification scheme. The United States faced the problem of how to classify some of the Iraqi opposition groups that it had supported, or the Lebanese militant group, Hezbollah, that it opposes. Most in the Middle East deny that Hezbollah is a terrorist organization because its primary targets have been Israeli soldiers on Lebanese soil. America can disregard the arguments of other states and target whichever terrorist enterprise it wants, but it would increasingly find itself alone in the pursuit of terrorists, an opening that such groups would exploit.

By focusing its efforts on identifying "terrorist groups," the United States may have missed an opportunity to rally members of the UN Security Council behind a clearer definition of "terrorism" as an instrument. A good example is the Hezbollah organization in Lebanon. If the United States seeks to mobilize other states and to demand that they end their support for Hezbollah because the United States defines it as a "terrorist organization," the strategy is unlikely to work. Regardless of the methods that Hezbollah employs, states such as Iran are unlikely to sever their relations with the group or to seek its destruction. In Lebanon, Hezbollah is a political party with significant support and several members in the parliament. It is also a religious movement with deep religious links with Iran. Its stated objective of forcing

Israel out of the occupied Arab territories is accepted and applauded in much of the Middle East beyond Iran, and many in the region consider its methods, which have largely focused on attacking Israeli soldiers on Lebanese soil, not to be "terrorism." Hence it is difficult, if not impossible, to envision full regional cooperation if the American aim is to confront the group and eliminate all support for it. On the other hand, if American efforts focus on defeating "terrorist means" defined as the deliberate targeting of civilians, the United States would have a better chance of succeeding. If the United States rallies the international community to apply the principle universally, it stands a good chance of persuading other states to pressure Hezbollah and dissuade it from using terrorist instruments and to delegitimize those instruments even inside Lebanon.

The United States had alternatives: first, to work with the United Nations and other international and regional organizations to pass resolutions prohibiting the targeting of civilians and strengthening existing norms that hold a state accountable for criminal acts committed by terrorists operating from its territory. Second, it could build on the antiterrorist coalition it had rallied to create a comprehensive new treaty regime—going beyond the existing patchwork of agreements that require individual states to either prosecute or extradite terrorists by mandating a strong collective response to attacks on civilians. Such a response targeting both the perpetrators and the states that support them could take various forms, including intelligence sharing, asset freezes, economic sanctions, expulsion from international organizations, and criminal prosecution. In this way a deliberate attack on civilian targets in one state would become an attack on all. States outside the coalition could ratify the treaty.

Such a treaty would not take away a state's right to self-defense when attacked but would add an obligation to take collective action. The difference is this: When you attack a state, you are at war with that state and its allies; when you deliberately attack civilians, you are at war with the entire international community and deserve an automatic international response. While there will always be ambiguities, the deterrent power of a mandatory collective response should be considerably stronger than the threat of unilateral action by a nation attacked by terrorists. More important, by moving in this direction, the international community would go a long way toward delegitimizing the deliberate targeting of civilians by terrorists. And by focusing on targeting civilians, rather than on the identity or motivations of the perpetrators, we could avoid the difficult and divisive debates about what constitutes terrorism and about which groups are terrorist and which "freedom fighters."

It was clear that the disadvantage of a multilateral approach would be that it would constrain the American ability to identify terrorist groups and to prioritize which should be confronted first. This process was in part a function of the blurring of difference between "terrorists" and "enemies." It was as if when a group or a state were not identified as terrorist, the United States would lose its right to treat it as a hostile enemy. Certainly, whether or not Iran is labeled as a "terrorist state," the United States has a right to regard it as an enemy and to construct its policy toward it accordingly. The United States also has a right to treat Hezbollah, which has killed Americans, as an enemy—regardless of how others view this organization.

The unilateral U.S. approach to identifying terrorist groups beyond al-Qaeda was bolstered by the early success in destroying the Taliban regime in Afghanistan. The surprisingly easy achievement seemed to confirm the view that America can go it alone in the era of the single superpower. The impressive performance by high-tech weapons enabled the speedy conduct of a war in a remote and difficult land that had defeated even the mighty Soviet army next door. The awareness that the collapse of the Soviet Union has only widened the gap in military technology between the United States and the rest of the world emboldened those who believe that America can afford to act alone. Nowhere has this attitude been more clearly visible than in the U.S. debate about the policy toward Saddam Hussein's Iraq, where the White House and Pentagon instinct was to prepare for a war to topple the government of Saddam Hussein even as most states around the world rejected the idea. The unilateralists had a ready argument: Because America is so powerful, few would oppose it if it decided to act even if they did not like its actions. No one could afford to be on the losing side, and America was ultimately assured of winning. Regardless of the actual merits of this argument, it is not hard to see that such an approach would engender anything but significant international resentment.

2. The Supply and Demand Sides of Terrorism

A second reason for the gap between the United States and much of the rest of the world is in the way the United States approached the terrorism phenomenon. By regarding terrorism as the product of organized groups that could be confronted and destroyed, without regard to their aims or to the reasons that they succeed in recruiting many willing members, the United States pursued a "supply-side"-only approach.

It is clear that the White House view of terrorism was colored by the 9/11 attacks. It was hard, in the state in which Americans found themselves, to contemplate the thought that the horror could be rationally explained. It is often feared that to explain is to justify. It is an understandable fear that is also ultimately self-defeating. In explaining such actions, one hopes to reduce the chance of more horror.

It is certainly the case that Usama bin Laden's al-Qaeda, even aside from its tactics of violent terror, has objectives that are irreconcilable not only with what America stands for but also with the state system as it now exists in the Middle East. It seeks to destabilize the system, to overthrow governments in the region, to fashion an Islamist political order to its liking. It is hard to see how one can reduce the threat of this organization without seeking its disruption. It is a supplier of terror that must be directly confronted.

But aside from the aims of bin Laden and other al-Qaeda leaders, there is a "demand side" to terrorism. To succeed, terror organizers, regardless of their aims, need to recruit willing members, raise funds, and appeal to public opinion in pursuit of their political objectives. Public despair and humiliation are often fertile ground for terror organizers to exploit. If this demand side persists, the terrorism phenomenon is unlikely to be contained. For every terror organization that is destroyed, other suppliers will arise to exploit the persistent demand.

It is important to note that there need not be harmony between the real aims of terror organizers and the causes of despair and humiliation that give rise to the demand side. Usama bin Laden's aims, for example, were fundamentally focused on expelling foreign forces from Saudi Arabia and creating an Islamic political order across the Muslim world. But once Usama bin Laden needed to rally public opinion in the region in the aftermath of 9/11, he did not employ his grand objectives as the primary arguments for mobilizing support. Instead, he highlighted issues that resonate with the public and that explain more fully the sense of despair and humiliation among Arabs and Muslims: the Arab-Israeli issue and sanctions against Iraq. Put differently, it is difficult to envision how one can address the terrorism phenomenon without addressing the central issues that create the fertile grounds for breeding terrorism and are exploited by organizers who may have ambitions of their own. Much of the world sees the U.S. war on terrorism as being limited to a military campaign against suppliers without investing in the necessary political and economic instruments to reduce the central demand side.

3 Terrorism as an Instrument Versus Terrorism as an Ideology

President Bush's speech to the American people a few days after the attacks, on September 20, 2001, was forceful and inspiring. It helped Americans begin dealing with their pain and fear. But in rallying the public for the declared war on terrorism and preparing it for the required cost, the speech eloquently addressed terrorism as another "ism" of history and of terrorists as ideologues: "They are the heirs of all the murderous ideologies of the twentieth century . . . they follow in the path of fascism, and Nazism, and totalitarianism. And they will follow that path all the way to where it ends: in history's unmarked grave of discarded lies." Although this approach succeeded in mobilizing public support in America, it soon became clear that others around the world see the terrorism phenomenon differently. The differences are especially consequential for policy.

In the ensuing months, the Bush administration has been waging the global war on terrorism as if terrorism is a movement, an ideology, or a political coalition, with little differentiation between cases. This approach has distorted our moral view of the world and enabled even Slobodan Milosevic, the former Yugoslav president, as he faced international justice, to justify his horrific policies of death and ethnic cleansing as a war on terrorism.

Much of the world sees terrorism differently: as an instrument, not a movement; as an immoral means employed by groups, some of which have just causes, some of which don't.

To reduce its occurrence, according to this approach, terrorism must be internationally delegitimized and the conditions under which it thrives minimized. By definition, legitimacy and illegitimacy cannot be unilaterally decided; when the United States appears to go against the rest of the world, it is its actions that appear illegitimate.

The argument against terrorism is essentially moral: To dissuade others from using such tactics, one has to speak with moral authority. Those with legitimate causes who condone terrorism as a method to serve their ends see terrorism as a weapon of the weak and helpless facing a far stronger enemy. Certainly, those in the Middle East who have often supported operations by Palestinian groups against Israelis, including attacks against civilians, regard those operations not as terrorism but as acts of national liberation. This perspective has been a central point of contention between the United States and many individuals and entities in the region, including governments. Many in the Middle East as well as in other parts of the world make the point that the definition of terrorism cannot be fully divorced from the degree to which the aim of the group is legitimate, and from the degree to which the power of the enemy it faces is overwhelmingly superior. Terrorism is seen as the weapon of the desperate and weak.

This notion should be challenged, as the United States has been trying to do: Terrorist means must be rejected regardless of their aims. But any successful effort to reduce the appeal of terrorism must also persuade people and groups not of the illegitimacy of their cause but of the illegitimacy of their means. The argument is moral: The ends, no matter how worthy, cannot justify the means. In particular, the argument boils down to the notion that the deliberate attack on civilian targets is unacceptable under any circumstances.

But to persuade others of this worthy notion, those who make the argument must speak with moral authority. And for the argument to be more persuasive, others with moral authority must also use it. This tactic requires an appeal to societies, and it requires multilateral efforts to establish the notion of the illegitimacy of terrorist means. But the understandable focus on destroying al-Qaeda, and the focus on terrorists as a breed that can be separated from society, has undermined the American ability to delegitimize terrorism. One of the unfortunate products of what transpired in the months after 9/11 is that whereas terrorist organizations, especially al-Qaeda, have been disrupted, terrorist means are increasingly legitimate in the eyes of more people in the Middle East.

A good case in point occurred as the United States was attempting to encourage Arab governments to speak against terrorism carried out by Palestinian groups in Israel following a spate of horrific suicide bombings that killed many in the spring of 2002. This was an important and worthy American effort consistent with the moral notion that the ends cannot justify such horrible means. The U.S. efforts intensified after major Israeli incursions into Palestinian cities in the West Bank that led to dozens of civilian casualties and much destruction of property. Both the suicide bombings and the Israeli operations were universally criticized, especially by human rights groups that saw severe violations of international law and norms that killed and injured many civilians. The Bush administration's focus only on the need to respond to terrorist attacks hindered its ability to emphasize the moral limits that must also be imposed on the response. The American obligation to project empathy with the innocent casualties on the Palestinian side was forgotten. As a result, the ability of the United States to persuade peoples and governments in the Middle East to effectively reject terrorism was significantly undermined.

In justifying the American demand that Israel should withdraw from Palestinian cities without delay, President Bush spoke only of possible "consequences" of continued Israeli operations but not of the moral wrong of the unjustified scale and scope of Israeli operations and the means Israel had used. In asking Israel to withdraw after a week of its military campaign in the West Bank, the president argued on April 4, 2002, that the situation in which Palestinian leader Yasser Arafat found himself "is largely of his own making." He put his request this way: "Israel is facing a terrible and serious challenge. For seven days, it has acted to root out terrorist nests. America recognizes Israel's right to defend itself from terror. Yet, to lay the foundations of future peace, I ask Israel to halt incursions into Palestinian-controlled areas and begin the withdrawal from those cities it has recently occupied."

In our approach to the Palestinian-Israeli conflict, we have taken a clear moral position toward Palestinian terrorism that goes like this: The Palestinians must be restrained in their response to the hardship that they endure daily after thirty-five years of occupation and to the humiliation that an entire generation experiences today. Although they have a right to seek freedom, they have no right to use terrorist tactics that inflict so much horror on many innocent people. The ends can never justify the means. This is a worthy moral position.

Then we turn to the Israelis as we watch the horror that they endure in the face of suicide bombings. We understand that they must respond in some way, but we act as if they can respond in any way they choose. We do not impose the moral limitations of demanding such actions must not be sweeping, that they must be less hurtful to the hundreds of thousands of innocent Palestinians who suffer the consequences. In fact, we take no moral position and appear to give a blank check. Our global moral authority is undermined as a result.

In the process, the ability of regional governments to help delegitimize terrorism is also undermined. During the same bloody events in April 2002, for example, the president asked Arab leaders to speak out against terrorism. He dispatched Secretary of State Colin Powell to visit friendly Arab states, including Jordan and Egypt, with the hope that they would issue such statements in Powell's presence. The trouble was that television stations in the region, over which these governments often have little control, were broadcasting live the destruction in West Bank cities, tanks rolling over houses, and heartbreaking reports of dozens of civilian casualties—even as television reports in Israel focused on the innocent victims of terrorist bombings. Hundreds of thousands of people demonstrated in the Arab world, including one million in Morocco. Callers and commentators on television shows blamed America for its inability to stop the campaign and for not displaying sympathy with Arab pain. They labeled Arab leaders friendly to the United States, such as President Mubarak of Egypt and King Abdullah of Jordan, as "servants of America." Regardless of the merits of these feelings and perceptions, when Arab leaders criticized Palestinian terrorism in that environment in response to public American pressure, they further delegitimized themselves rather than terrorism.

Whereas we ignored the moral dimension of Israeli actions, we chose to evaluate Palestinian behavior *only* in that dimension. This bias has handicapped our ability to perceive the need to put forth serious political alternatives to violence even as we rightly demand that terrorism must stop. Terrorism cannot be justified under any circumstances, but it is more likely to take root when peaceful alternatives to alleviating hardship are not readily available. Any successful strategy to minimize terrorism must include putting forth a positive alternative. To pretend that the issue of terrorism is simply a choice between good and evil is to know nothing of human psychology. In 2002, nearly half of Israelis supported the immoral notion of expelling all Palestinians from their homes as a way of stopping the unbearable horror of suicide terror because they saw no peaceful solution on the horizon, and many Palestinians supported terror as a way of ridding themselves of the unbearable pain of occupation. This was

This is not to say that states have no role in supporting violent groups outside their own borders, but violence, including terrorism, is more likely to emanate from weakened states, even without support from outside powers. Afghanistan provides a good example. During the days of Soviet occupation, the communist government in Afghanistan was less likely to export terrorism than Afghanistan was in the years that followed the disintegration of that state and the emergence of the Taliban regime. Violence is easier to deter when it emanates from states that maintain strong domestic control than when it is nurtured in weak or collapsing states.

This contrast suggests important aspects of a strategy intended to reduce terrorism. The first is that when confronting hostile states, such as Iraq, any strategy must assure an outcome that does not produce the sort of instability that is hospitable to terrorism. Second, it is not enough to limit the opportunities available to potential terrorist groups—the issue of motivation is also central. Even if opportunities for terrorism become limited through effective military means, the degree to which people are driven to extremes affects the likelihood that they will succeed. When there is a will, there is a way.

5. Gap in Understanding Middle Eastern Terror

The Role of Religion. Understandably, the attacks of September 11 have raised many questions about the motivation of those willing to commit such atrocities against the United States. Inevitably, a debate ensued about the relationship between Islam as a religion and culture and the propensity to commit terror. After all, those who carried out the attacks and their sponsors professed to be fulfilling a religious mission.

One of the most important positions taken by President Bush in the early days following the horror was his attempt to set the record straight, to differentiate between those few terrorists and Muslims broadly. This important position helped not only in enabling cooperation between the United States and Muslim countries that were equally frightened by al-Qaeda but also to reduce the backlash in America against Muslim and Arab Americans.

However, despite these attempts, the discourse in America quickly blurred the distinction. When the question of "why they hate us so much" was raised, "they" increasingly meant Arabs and Muslims, not merely those individuals who carried out the attack. In some quarters the mood was even more dramatic: The editor of the influential conservative *National Review,* Rich Lowry, openly discussed the option of "nuking Mecca" if there is another large terrorist attack on the United States, though he also acknowledged that such an attack "seems extreme." The prominent commentator Fred Ikle, a former undersecretary of defense, concluded an op-ed article in *The Wall Street Journal* (June 2, 2002) this way: "A nuclear war stirred up against the 'infidels' might end up displacing Mecca and Medina with two large radioactive craters." Although these writings were by no means the norm in America, they were highlighted in the Muslim and Arab worlds as if they were American policy, thus generating more resentment toward the United States. In the logic of these writers, the issue was how to deter future attacks and the right of the United States to retaliate in case of such attacks; from the point of view of Muslims worldwide, such writings confused the actions of a few radical Muslims with the Muslim faith and conceived of Islam, not the terrorists, as America's enemy.

At the heart of this analytical confusion is a genuine fear that followed the nightmare of watching the horrific attacks as they occurred. It was hard to explain how anyone could be ruthless enough to design and carry out such horror, but the revelations about the perpetrators made the situation even more terrifying: They were willing to die for the cause and thus were seemingly insensitive to punishment and reward; many were apparently normal men who were relatively well educated and came from middle-class families; and they had undertaken their mission in the name of Islam, a religion most Americans knew little about. It is frightening to contemplate confronting ruthless people, but it is even more terrifying to envision them as mysterious and irrational. This seeming mystery of their behavior was easy to account for psychologically by references to blind religious faith, especially when it happens that many of those carrying out terrorist acts in the Middle East, not just al-Qaeda, are doing so in the name of Islam.

But an analytical view of the behavior of groups that carry out terror, especially in historical perspective, clearly indicates that Islam as such is not at the heart of the propensity to commit such acts. Even the seemingly incomprehensible phenomenon of using suicide as an instrument of violence can be accounted for without reference to religion. This is not to say that religion plays no role, or that many Islamist groups are not dangerous or hostile, but only that religion's role is not the central issue in understanding the terror phenomenon. What makes these groups dangerous is not their Islamic character but their violent means and intolerant ends. In contrast, most religious organizations, including political ones in the Middle East, are not violent. There is nothing wrong with religious fundamentalism (whatever the religion); what's wrong is when a group, religious or otherwise, seeks to impose its will on others through violence.

One of the most radical Palestinian groups in the Middle East in the late 1960s was the Popular Front for the Liberation of Palestine (PFLP), a secular organization founded by a Christian physician, George Habash. The PFLP, which engaged in a series of highly publicized airline hijackings, attracted many well-educated members. The secularism of this group should be a reminder of the mistaken assumptions many make about the relationship between the Islamic religion and violence. It is true that religious groups employing violence find some theological justification for it, just as their opponents find support for their positions in religious materials. But "theological justification" is not the same thing as "religiously caused." The Jonestown cult did not represent Christianity any more than Baruch Goldstein and his supporters represented Judaism. It is telling that when the violence in the Middle East was carried out by secular nationalists in the 1950s and 1960s, both the West and intellectuals in the region saw Islam as a passive religion, an "opiate of the masses" that accepted the status quo and bolstered stability. The prevalent interpretation was that a Muslim simply accepted God's will and did not seek to change it, repeating the phrase "al-Hamdulillah" (Praise be to God) even in the face of great hardship.

During that period the United States and the West viewed secular national movements in the Middle East as the primary destabilizing political force in the region and viewed Islamic groups, especially those supported by friendly governments, as more desirable and more stabilizing. The Israelis held a similar view after they occupied the West Bank and Gaza in the 1967 war. They perceived the secular Palestine Liberation Organization (PLO) as the primary threat to Israel, so they sought to erode its influence in the West Bank and Gaza and consequently encouraged traditional Islamic groups that were competing with the PLO. Those same Islamic groups ultimately gave birth to Hamas and Islamic Jihad, two militant movements that were even more ruthless in their use of violence than the PLO.

Similarly, it is important to keep in mind Usama bin Laden's political roots. In the 1980s, when the fear of communism and the Soviet Union still superseded all other perceived threats, the mission of overthrowing the Soviet-backed communist regime in Afghanistan propelled the United States to cultivate Islamic groups across the world to fight the regime in Afghanistan. The United States encouraged these efforts in the name of jihad, or Islamic struggle, in order to persuade Muslim fighters in places as far away as Saudi Arabia, Egypt, and the Sudan to join in this global struggle against the infidel communists. Indeed, the Saudi government was encouraged to help locate fanatically religious people like Usama bin Laden, especially wealthy ones. The recruitment of global adherents of Islam to fight what these believers defined as holy wars, a phenomenon that obviously had unintended horrific consequences, was thus born of a different interpretation of Islam. The role that many Arab governments played in mobilizing Islamists, for which they are now criticized, was born in part out of this collaborative effort with the United States. It is thus not surprising that most of those who have carried out attacks against the United States have been citizens of friendly states such as Saudi Arabia and Egypt rather than hostile states such as Iran or Iraq.

Outside the al-Qaeda phenomenon, it is important to note that Middle Eastern terrorism and the resentment of the United States, unacceptable as they remain, are not unique if examined in global perspective. If one sets aside al-Qaeda as a horrific special case, one will find the global trends in terrorism to be surprising. According to State Department reports, and contrary to conventional wisdom, the Middle East was not the leading region in the number of terrorist incidents (as defined and identified by the State Department) throughout the 1990s.[1] Nor has it been the leading area in the number of attacks against American targets. In fact, in the five years prior to the horror of 9/11, incidents of Middle

Eastern terrorism declined every year, and by 2000 the Middle East had become the region with the fewest terrorist attacks of any around the globe except North America. In countering the tendency to associate Islam with terror, one must keep this global trend in mind.

Religion and Suicide Terrorism. The mystery of suicide attacks was compounded by the discovery that many of the al-Qaeda attackers were well educated and from middle-class families. This information seemed to go against the popular notion that participants in political violence come from the uneducated and economically destitute classes. There is actually little evidence that poverty or lack of education are major elements in political violence, although they can be factors in extreme cases. The more central reasons motivating people to act, and to be recruited by violent groups, are hopelessness and humiliation, which have to do with expectations and interpretations of social and political relations. These factors are essential in defining the "demand side" of terrorism.

Historically, those who have employed violence for political ends have come from the educated and middle classes—whether in the Middle East or elsewhere. Often seeing themselves as revolutionaries, as in the case of Marxists such as Che Guevara in Latin America, or George Habash of the Popular Front for the Liberation of Palestine, the more educated segments of the public are generally less accepting of an inferior position in politics and society and are also more aware of their capacity to effect change. They are thus more likely to act on their beliefs, although most use nonviolent means.

One of the seemingly most puzzling aspects of the terrorist attacks on the United States was the use of suicide. It is easy, in this case, to escape the need to explain such apparently ir-rational behavior by focusing on Islamic theology—but there are rational explanations. First, theology cannot explain sui-cide as a method of terrorism, though the perpetrators and their supporters may have twisted religion to suit their ends and to brush aside the basic Islamic doctrine prohibiting sui-cide. One could just as easily create twisted biblical interpre-tations to justify the creation of a Christian or Jewish cult that exploits the biblical story of Samson's death.

Second, if it is assumed that Muslims do not fear death be-cause they believe they will be rewarded in heaven and therefore are more likely than others to accept dying, we needed to look no further than our television screens in the lead-up to the American military operations in Afghanistan: Hundreds of thousands of faithful Muslims tried to flee Afghanistan in fear for their lives. Bin Laden's own recruit-ment tapes that he distributes in the Arab world show that his primary means of motivating his supporters is to show pictures of dead Muslims in Palestine, Iraq, and Chechnya to move his audience into action.

Third, suicide bombings have not been unique to Islamic groups, either historically or recently. Certainly the suicide bombers in the Middle East in recent years have come from Islamist groups, and they do employ the concept of martyrdom to explain and justify their actions. But it is often forgotten that the PFLP and other militant secular Palestinian groups (which included Christians) in the 1950s and 1960s were called *fedayeen,* or those who sacrifice their lives. Historically, other groups and people have employed suicide, such as the Japanese in World War II. Although the focus on the Middle East is understandable, what's overlooked is that the Tamil Tigers in Sri Lanka, who are neither Arab nor Muslim, and who describe themselves as "a national liberation organization . . . [who] are not [so] mentally demented as to commit blind acts of violence impelled by racist and religious fanaticism"[2] have employed suicide bombings as an instrument of violence more than any other group in the world, including in the Middle East.

Ultimately, suicide bombings are employed by violent groups for two reasons: They are *effective,* and they are *empowering.* From the perspective of individual actors, suicide as a method is strictly irrational; from the point of view of a ruthless group, it is terrifyingly efficient. Bin Laden's organization must be seen as a cult because its method of persuasion is akin to brainwashing, although any person willing to die has individual reasons, and some, including secularists, as has been documented in the Palestinian case, actively seek organizations to help them carry out suicide attacks. When a group is willing to employ ruthless methods and to kill on a large scale, the sacrifice of group members is a horrifyingly effective tactic because it is very difficult to defend against. It is difficult to deter or punish individuals who are willing to die, and it is nearly impossible to stop episodes of terrorism if individuals are willing to use their bodies as weapons. In that sense, the seeming irrationality of suicide violence (i.e., its seeming insensitivity to punishment and reward) renders it a rational strategy from the point of view of those already willing to commit ruthless acts of violence. Even from the point of view of total casualties, the group will lose fewer fighters and inflict more casualties on its enemies than if it used means such as guerrilla warfare.

The horrific effectiveness of suicide bombings, especially against superior enemies, becomes a central factor in attracting new recruits. In the Palestinian arena in the West Bank and Gaza, the suicide-bombing method began with Islamist groups, Hamas and Islamic Jihad. By the spring of 2002, and in the absence of a hopeful political process to alleviate public despair over the conditions of occupation, secularist groups were having more difficulty competing with Islamist groups in the recruitment of members. Thus, they began emulating the suicide method as the PFLP and the al-Aqsa Martyrs' Brigade—two secular organizations—began to employ this method, even dispatching women bombers, a practice the Islamist groups were reluctant to accept. The suicide-bombing phenomenon has thus become secularized.

It is necessary to understand that suicide bombings, offensive though they are and ultimately threatening to the very societies that legitimize them, are also inspiring to many. The true horror of suicide bombings is that they are immensely empowering to many people who no longer believe that their governments can do anything to relieve their humiliation and improve their conditions. The fact that more groups, including secular ones, now employ this strategy is the result, not the cause, of popular support for a method first embraced by Islamist groups.

This message of empowerment is well understood by organizations that employ suicide bombings. When a teenaged Palestinian girl suicide bomber left a taped message in March 2002 speaking of "sleeping Arab armies" and ineffective governments allowing girls to do the fighting, her handlers knew well how the recording would play among the masses. The most pervasive psychology in the Arab world today is collective rage and feelings of helplessness—and the focus of this psychology is the continued bloodshed in the Palestinian-Israeli conflict.

In this climate, suicide bombings take root because they free the desperate from the need to rely on governments. Rather than being sponsored by states, this form of violence challenges states. Whatever the aims of the attacks on the United States, they succeeded in sending an empowering message to those in the Middle East who are frustrated but are seemingly resigned to their fate because of the superior strength of their enemies and their apparent helplessness. Though there were many in that region, especially among governments and elites, who were threatened by bin Laden and by the phenomenon that he represented, many among the public were inspired by what was accomplished: A few men with nothing but box cutters had succeeded in inflicting so much pain on the sole remaining superpower and in shaking the international order. In so doing, they were also bound to create change in the Middle East, even if the nature of that change remained unpredictable. Even if al-Qaeda itself is ultimately defeated, others are likely to emulate its methods.

In the end, it should be clear that the issues of political violence broadly and terrorism specifically are not about religion and theology. But it is undeniable that much of the politically militant action today is carried out by Islamist groups in the name of Islam and that these groups are on the ascent, even as nonreligious groups also continue to employ violent means. The question is why? The answer is hardly mysterious: In the absence of democracy and legitimate means for organizing political opposition, people turn to social organizations that are not fully under governmental control, and the mosque is one of the few available vehicles for mass political mobilization. This point highlights a key dilemma in the effort to reduce terror: On one extreme, very weak central authority allows militant organizations to proliferate and be less sensitive to deterrence; on the other extreme, significant repression increases the motives of individuals and groups to use violence and to take greater risks. Repression alone cannot eliminate terrorism and may even help cultivate it. This has been the experience of many Middle Eastern states, especially for Israel in its occupation of the West Bank and Gaza. Any successful counterterrorism strategy must thus address both the opportunities available to militants and the level of their motivation.

Besides limiting the opportunities open to organizers, any effective strategy must also include two essential components: (1) working with the international community, especially through international treaties, to delegitimize attacks on civilians as a political instrument and suicide attacks as something to be celebrated; and (2) addressing the demand side, the legitimate anger and genuine political despair in the Middle East today that provide fertile ground for terrorists to exploit. As in the 1990s, when the United States worked with the regional players to begin a credible process of resolving regional conflict through negotiations and put forth ideas for economic development and political change, a new process that inspires hope must be part of any new strategy. Unless we address the roots of this anger and despair, new terrorists taking advantage of public hopelessness could replace the ones we destroy.

There are profound reasons, with regard both to domestic policy and to foreign policy issues, especially the Arab-Israeli conflict, for people in the Middle East to be motivated to oppose the existing order. Despair and humiliation are widespread in the region. People turn to available vehicles of political organization, sometimes conveniently, sometimes instinctively. Such despair is the demand side of terrorism: Terrorists who have their own aims, including personal ambition or greed, can exploit this mood to recruit members, gain financial support, and show a public that may be resigned to its condition that change is possible. It is therefore important to understand the issues at the heart of the pervasive sense of humiliation in much of the region and to come to grips with why much of the anger is directed at the United States specifically. It is also important to ask: Why should we care? What's at stake for the United States in the Middle East today? These issues will be the subject of the following chapters.

2

"Why Do They
Hate Us So Much?"

They hate what we see right here in this chamber—a
democratically elected government. . . . They hate our
freedoms—our freedom of religion, our freedom of
speech, our freedom to vote and assemble and disagree
with each other. . . . These terrorists kill not merely to
end lives, but to disrupt and end a way of life.

—PRESIDENT GEORGE W. BUSH,
SEPTEMBER 20, 2001

President Bush's statements about the aims of the terrorists
before a joint session of Congress after the attacks on American soil resonated well with a nation seeking proof of its
strengths and its identity and rallying to confront a horrific
enemy. They also helped preempt an instinct that was in-

evitable given the magnitude of the American tragedy: to lash out in almost any way, to relieve the pain through almost any means. It was a reminder that what makes terrorism unacceptable is that no ends, even noble ones, can justify the horrific means that terrorists employ. It was an admonition that despite the overwhelming pain Americans felt, our hearts must never be so hardened as to forget that what was at stake was much bigger than mere retaliation and that we could not defend our values by subverting them.

Beyond this important mission, there was also truth in the proposition that bin Laden himself, and al-Qaeda broadly, sought to target America for what it stood for. Al-Qaeda advocated an intolerant world order in which there was no room for those who did not adhere to its fanatical views, even as it also opposed American policies toward the Middle East and the Islamic world, including the presence of U.S. forces in Saudi Arabia. The clash between al-Qaeda and much of the world was ultimately a clash of values and worldviews as well as policies. Although this is true of al-Qaeda, it is clearly not true that resentments toward American policies in Arab and Muslim countries are at heart a reflection of a clash of values. This distinction between bin Laden's mission and the sources of resentment of America in the Middle East, which the president and many congressional leaders attempted to make in the early days after 9/11, became quickly blurred in the national debate.

Increasingly in our national public discourse, when people asked, "Why do they hate us so much?" what they meant by "they" was Arabs and Muslims in general, not just those who had carried out the attacks on America. In part, this tendency could be easily explained. Besides the claim of al-Qaeda and its leaders to be speaking in the name of Muslims worldwide, there was also strong evidence that the public in the Middle East especially, and in the Muslim world overall, resented America even in its moment of tragedy. There was more sympathy with bin Laden than Americans had hoped, and many among the Muslim public opposed America's war on Afghanistan. Some hateful commentators, including many in positions of religious authority, uttered words reflecting the notion that a conflict of values was the central issue. A thesis that had been advanced years earlier by Professor Samuel Huntington of Harvard University, that the world was on a course toward a "clash of civilization," especially between the world of Islam and the West, quickly gained significant momentum.

Global Perceptions of America

While the danger exists that such a clash could indeed develop, the absence of a global perspective on how the world looks at America today could help turn the "clash of civilizations" thesis into a self-fulfilling prophecy. It is thus important to put the views Arabs and Muslims hold of the United States in broader global context. What becomes quickly evident is that many of the negative views that people in the Middle East and the Muslim world express about America are widely shared in other parts of the world. There are some issues that

are unique to Arabs and Muslims and require specific explanations, but the Middle East does not stand out on many issues that define global perceptions of America.

Indeed, a task force of the nonpartisan Council on Foreign
Relations that had been convened to address the need for
more active American public diplomacy summarized its
findings about the way the world views America as follows:

> Of course, foreign perceptions of the United States are far
> from monolithic. But there is little doubt that stereotypes of
> the United States as arrogant, self-indulgent, hypocritical,
> inattentive, and unwilling or unable to engage in cross-cultural
> dialogue are deeply rooted. In the eyes of some people,
> Americans largely ignored terrorism as a problem—remem-
> ber how quickly we forgot the 1993 attack on the World Trade
> Center—until the enormity of September 11 hit us.[1]

Some of these attitudes were reflected in surveys that have
been conducted globally since the attacks on the United
States. One of the most striking findings is the common perception that American foreign policy is unilateral and that
the wars on terrorism and Iraq have been conducted to serve
only America's interests, without taking into account the interests even of friends and allies. The perception of American unilateralism was also widespread in Europe, before and
after the attacks of 9/11. In August 2001, a poll published by
the *International Herald Tribune*[2] and conducted by the Pew
Research Center for the People and the Press in association
with the Council on Foreign Relations, found that majorities

of Europeans believed that American foreign policy disregards their interests. Of those polled, 79 percent in Britain, 74 percent in Italy, 73 percent in Germany, and 85 percent in France felt that President Bush "makes decisions based entirely on U.S. interests," without regard to their interests or those of their countries.

These findings were consistent with the outcome of a Gallup poll released in April 2002.[3] Majorities in four European countries expressed the view that the United States does not take allied interests into account in conducting the war on terrorism and that the United States acts in its own interest in the fight against terrorism (85 percent of Germans, 80 percent of French, 73 percent of British, and 68 percent of Italian respondents). Remarkably, the view of American unilateralism is shared by many people in the United States: In the same survey, 41 percent of Americans agreed that the United States acts unilaterally, without taking the interests of its allies into account.

These widespread global views went beyond public opinion. Fernando Henrique Cardoso, the president of Brazil and a prominent sociologist, declared before the French National Assembly in Paris on October 30, 2001 that "barbarism is not only the cowardliness of terrorism but also the intolerance or imposition of unilateral policies on a global scale."[4]

While many *governments* around the world lent support for the American war in Afghanistan in its early stages, including even unfriendly states such as Iran, opposition to the war among the *public* was by no means limited to the Arab and Muslim world and was prevalent in the developing world, especially in Latin America and Africa. Of eleven Latin American countries surveyed by Gallup in November and December 2001,[5] majorities in ten opposed the war in Afghanistan, including 76 percent in Argentina, 73 percent in Mexico, and 72 percent in Bolivia. Majorities in three of four African countries surveyed also opposed the war.

Even on questions pertaining to American policy on the Middle East, the direction of global opinion was similar to the direction of opinion expressed in the Middle East. Certainly, people in the Middle East have questioned American policy in the region, strongly opposed a new war with Iraq, and felt that U.S. policy in the Middle East favors Israel at their expense. Whatever conclusions might be reached by an objective assessment of U.S. policy, these perceptions are widely shared around the world.

In western Europe, for example, majorities expressed a decidedly negative reaction to President Bush's labeling of Iraq, Iran, and North Korea as "the axis of evil." There was solid opposition to a U.S.-led military operation against Iraq in places such as Germany and Italy. Even in Britain, where support for the United States is strong, a poll published by the *Mail* on August 4, 2002, showed that majorities opposed war with Iraq and believed that Prime Minister Tony Blair was behaving like President Bush's "poodle." Criticism of broader U.S. policy in the Middle East was widespread in every region around the world, including western Europe.

On the Arab-Israeli issue—which is closest to the hearts of many people in the Middle East and draws a significant part

of the criticism of U.S. policy—polls show consistent negative sentiments toward the United States in regions around
the world. In western Europe, for example, where there is a
pervasive sense that U.S. policy toward the Arab-Israeli conflict is biased, more express sympathy with the Palestinians
than with Israel. In general, majorities of Europeans sympa-
thize with neither side, but those who do take sides favor the
Palestinians more. Remarkably, in a poll conducted in
France by Zogby in spring 2002,[6] 70 percent of respondents
said they would react more favorably toward the United
States if it "were to apply pressure to ensure the creation of
an independent Palestinian state."

Interestingly, the European views of the Arab-Israeli conflict are echoed in some ways by the views of the American
public. Almost all polls show that most Americans favor neither the Israelis nor the Palestinians. Of the minorities who
do take sides, most favor Israel. But on policy issues, there
are decided differences between the views of the American
public and U.S. policy toward the Middle East. Congress, for
example, overwhelmingly passed a resolution in May 2002
expressing unequivocal support for Israel's military actions
and stating that "the United States and Israel are now engaged in a common struggle against terrorism." At the very
same time, a poll conducted by the Program on International Policy Attitudes[7] at the University of Maryland
showed that only 17 percent of the respondents said that Israel's struggle with the Palestinians was best understood as a
Mideast version of the war on terrorism. The same poll
showed that a large majority of Americans want American

foreign policy to be "even-handed" and don't think that it has in fact been even-handed.

Hence it is important to begin any study of the attitudes of Arabs and Muslims toward the United States by remembering that on many issues, especially those having to do with American foreign policy, these attitudes do not appear significantly out of place in global context, whatever the reasons behind them.

Arab and Muslim Attitudes Toward the United States

One prevalent view of Arab and Muslim attitudes toward the United States was well expressed by an analyst testifying before the Foreign Affairs Committee of the House of Representatives at the end of the Gulf War in 1991: "I think that anger in the Arab street is real. It is produced by a number of different factors. But in the end, what matters is not whether they hate us or love us—for the most part, they hate us. They did before. But whether they are going to respect our power."[8] This view suggests that there has always been fundamental resentment of the United States and that such resentment is unlikely to change, and therefore the United States should do little to address the sources of resentment and focus instead on the employment of its power to achieve policy objectives. Whether or not public attitudes in the Middle East in particular, and around the globe in general, should be of concern to American policymakers is an important issue that will be addressed in the next chapter. For now, it is important to address the extent to which it is true that attitudes toward the United States have always been negative and to analyze the findings of the studies that have been conducted since September 2001.

Although it is true that there are many commonalities in the views of Arabs and Muslims, these views are by no means monolithic, and there are significant differences among Arabs and other Muslims, culturally, politically, geographically, and even religiously. It is also important to remember that, even in recent history, many Arab and Muslim governments in the region have had more in common politically with the United States than with each other. Obviously, the Gulf War in 1991 was an example of a U.S.-led coalition that included Muslim states in opposition to another largely Muslim state, Iraq. Moreover, the two states in the Muslim world that have ruled in the name of Islam more than any other in recent decades, Saudi Arabia and Iran, have had decidedly different foreign policies, with the former being an ally and the latter an adversary of the United States.

It is also important to remember that the West itself is not monolithic in the eyes of people in the Arab and Muslim countries. Although many speaking out in the public debate in the United States continue to define the sources of Arab and Muslim resentment of the United States as a profound opposition to "Western values," people in the Middle East in particular have decidedly different views of Western countries. A Gallup poll released in February 2002[9] showed, for example, that views of the United States are more unfavorable than favorable in all but one of the nine Muslim countries studied, while France received more favorable than unfavorable ratings in all but two countries. It is hard to make the case that these attitudes are therefore a reaction to "Western values" rather than policies.

Policies Versus Values

Certainly, a significant part of the resentment of the United States in the Middle East is based on American policies toward the region and perceived American aims. Some religious groups have historically objected to the importation of Western values into the Middle East and have felt especially threatened by the trend of secularization that Western-influenced nationalists have attempted to create. But polls today confirm what the history of the U.S. relationship with the Middle East indicates: that the sources of this resentment have more to do with issues of U.S. policy.

In two surveys I commissioned (with Zogby International) in Saudi Arabia in March 2002, this question was asked: "Are your frustrations with the United States mostly based on its policies or on its values?" In the survey of Saudi elites, 86 percent saw American policies as the source of their frustrations, and in the poll of the Saudi public, 59 percent identified "policies" as the cause, whereas 19 percent identified "values." This result was bolstered by the response of Saudis to another question about world leaders they admire most, outside Saudi Arabia. Among elites, the leading vote-getter was President Mubarak of Egypt (12 percent), followed by President Jacques Chirac of France (11 percent) and Mahathir Muhammad of Malaysia (10 percent) all of whom are Western or pro-Western leaders. Among the general public the leading vote-getters were the president of Syria, Bashar Assad (11 percent), President Mubarak (10 percent), and Muammar al-Qaddafi of Libya (9 percent)—all of whom are secular Arab nationalists. No significant support for any Islamist leader appeared among the elites, and the only Islamist receiving significant support among the public was Usama bin Laden (8 percent). In fact, "George Bush" (the respondents didn't indicate which Bush they meant) received 4 percent, which was more than Taliban leader Mullah Omar, Hamas leader Ahmad Yassin, and the religious authority Yusuf al-Qaradawi combined. In other words, the leading admired figures among both elites and the general public were all secular, not religious, leaders.

Though many in the region take issue with American and Western values more broadly, it is important to understand the source of their distaste. Surveys indicate that the dominant perception in Arab and Muslim countries is that religion and family are not important in America. Certainly, such values are central in Arab and Muslim countries. In a Gallup survey[10] of nine Muslim countries released in February 2002, respondents rated the importance in their lives of five institutions: religion, family, extended family, country, and "myself." Two of these categories—religion and family—were by far the most likely to be perceived as important. Having a comfortable economic life competed in perceived importance with having a rich religious or spiritual life in several countries—including Jordan, Saudi Arabia, Morocco, Kuwait, Turkey, Indonesia, and Lebanon, where economic comfort actually outranked religious or spiritual riches by a substantial margin.

Even though people in Muslim countries perceive religion and family as being unimportant in American life, Americans themselves have consistently ranked these values high in polls. But the perceptions in Muslim countries are largely based on the narrow prism through which they see the United States: television programs and movies that give the impression that Hollywood's values are America's values. Most know little else about American culture, and even in major centers of learning and universities, especially in the Arab world, there are few significant programs of American studies.

Despite the expression of disapproval of these perceived American values, some of these critics strive to live in America, readily watch the same American movies that they criticize, and enjoy consuming American products. In the Arab world in particular, there is much that most people like about American values. A Zogby International ten-nation survey showed that majorities of people in all five Arab countries included in the study had a favorable view of American "freedom and democracy." Majorities in all countries also looked favorably upon American movies, American products, and, importantly, American education.

In contrast to the views of aspects of American culture and values, in the same poll most people expressed negative views of American policies. Roughly a third in Arab and Muslim countries supported the war on terrorism, and only about 12 percent viewed American policy on Palestine favorably. Certainly there are some in the Muslim world, as in other parts of the world, who have intolerant views, who are racist, who hate Western values broadly. Even Americans are not unified regarding what their nation's values should be or about the role that religion should play in our society—not to mention the role that Hollywood values should play in American life. But the evidence is clear: The central issue behind the resentment that most hold toward the United States is not American values but American policies. It is thus important to begin with a brief overview of the evolution of America's relations with the Middle East.

A Historical Overview

Contemporary attitudes toward the United States and France are in decidedly marked contrast with the attitudes in the region toward Western powers in the first half of the twentieth century. Whereas Europeans had long-standing connections with the Middle East, the United States was geographically far removed from that region. As the European nations conspired to divide the spoils of World War I in the Middle East among themselves, U.S. President Woodrow Wilson dispatched the King-Crane Commission to the Middle East to inquire about the wishes of its people, in harmony with his strong advocacy of the right of self-determination. Ironically, the commissioners were told upon their visit to Syria, Lebanon, and Palestine in 1919 that, failing to achieve independence, the people there were prepared to accept the United States as their first choice for governing them through a mandate from the League of Nations. They overwhelmingly opposed France, except for a number of pro-French petitions from Lebanon.

In the end the European powers prevailed. The region's hopes for self-determination and independence were dashed as the Arab world was carved up to suit the interests of the European colonial powers, especially Britain and France. In addition, an Italian conquest of Libya began in 1911. Those colonial divisions formed the basis of the contemporary state system. They also left a scar on the region's psyche that was often invoked by Arab political movements seeking to reverse what they saw as unnatural divisions that had weakened a historically great people. Both the Arab secular nationalists, especially those led by Gamal Abdel Nasser of Egypt in the 1950s and 1960s, and Islamic political movements have often envisioned unifying the region in the name of Arabism or Islamism. Even Saddam Hussein of Iraq, who headed a secular Arab nationalist party, the Baath, attempted to portray himself as a sort of Bismarck of the Arab world who would redress the sense of weakness in the region through unification.

The political and military role of the United States in the Middle East increased significantly after the 1967 Arab-Israeli War. U.S. links with the region in the first half of the twentieth century were largely through trade, especially in oil, and cultural exchange, including the establishment of centers of learning such as the American University in Beirut. Public opinion of the United States in the Middle East was largely positive, in contrast with the continued tension between that region and the European powers, especially Britain and France, which lasted beyond World War II, even after the mandatory period of control ended.

After the Second World War, the role of the United States in the Middle East increased with the introduction of the Truman Doctrine in 1947 aimed at protecting Turkey and Greece, on the periphery of the region, from Soviet threats. But the defining cause of the Arab nationalist movement was anti-imperialism, by which was meant primarily British and French imperialism. Both Britain and France continued their presence in North Africa and the Persian Gulf for the next two decades. Both joined Israel in 1956 in the so-called Suez War against Egypt after Egypt's president, Gamal Abdel Nasser, nationalized the Suez Canal, in which the British government held a large minority share. It was America's opposition to that campaign by its European allies during the presidency of Dwight Eisenhower that ultimately forced Britain, France, and Israel to withdraw from Egypt.

The tension between the United States and Arab nationalist governments, especially in Egypt and Syria, increased in the following decade as those governments joined the movement of nonalignment and drew closer to the Soviet Union. The United States declared the Eisenhower Doctrine in 1957, aimed at deterring Soviet influence in the region, and later deployed American forces in Lebanon. But the Europeans continued to maintain a presence in the region and were the primary target of regional anger. The Persian Gulf, where the West had enormous interest in energy resources, was protected largely through the presence of British, not American, military bases. And Israel, which continued to receive political and economic support from the United States, relied almost entirely on French arms for its military forces. Its air force, which was crucial in winning the 1967 war with Egypt, Syria, and Jordan, was primarily supplied by France. In the decade between the Suez War and the 1967 war, Arabs were mostly engaged in their own cold war between the Egypt-led nationalists and the traditional conservative governments supported by the United States and the West, such as those in Saudi Arabia and Jordan.

The picture changed dramatically in the years following the 1967 war. The British began their final withdrawal from the Persian Gulf region, and the French stopped supplying arms to Israel. Also, the influence of the Soviet Union was increasing. The Soviets established bases in Egypt and consolidated relations with Iraq in the Persian Gulf. This environment, which the Nixon administration inherited, led to a new American role: replacing the European powers as the protector of Western interests against Soviet influence in the Middle East. The strategy seemed simple—support Israel and Iran militarily and politically and empower them to balance Iraq in the Gulf and Egypt and Syria in the Arab-Israeli arena. Along the way, the United States hoped to be able to contain Soviet influence, assure stability in the Gulf, and maintain support for Israel.

These objectives were partially attained in the short term. But a new view of the United States began to replace the old view in the regional psychology. America was increasingly filling the gap left by the European colonial powers by playing new roles that worked against regional aspirations: first, supporting conservative governments in the 1950s and 1960s against the popular tide of secular nationalism; then turning states that Arabs considered as enemies into powerful U.S. allies. These allies were Israel, which had been the central target of Arabs who aspired to help the Palestinians, and Iran, a non-Arab state that had long-standing conflicts with Iraq and the smaller Arab Gulf states. Whatever its objective merits, U.S. policy in the Middle East went against the aspirations of many for a more unified and powerful Arab world, progressive governments, justice for the Palestinians, and reduced foreign influence. The United States was increasingly seen as the anchor of an undesirable political order.

The 1967 war also changed the reality for the region. The defeat of Egypt in 1967 dashed the aspirations of the pan-Arab movement. The cold war among Arab states ended as they sought to deal with the psychology of a significant Arab defeat that led to the occupation of land in Egypt, Jordan, and Syria, including the West Bank, Gaza, and the Golan Heights. As the United States supported Israel with new, advanced military technology that trumped the weapons the Arabs received from the Soviet Union, the hope of recovering the lost territories by force diminished even as Egypt and Syria continued to plan for such a war. The United States saw no urgency in addressing the political demands that the

Arabs put forth, nor did it see a direct relationship between what transpired in the Arab-Israeli arena and the continued flow of oil at reasonable prices from the Persian Gulf. Certainly, the years between the 1967 and the 1973 Arab-Israeli wars witnessed mounting resentment toward the United States and its increasingly central role in the region. Indeed, after the death of President Nasser of Egypt in 1970, his successor, Anwar Sadat, was fond of saying "99 percent of the cards" were in the hands of the United States. Whether or not this proposition was true, the assumption that the United States held the key to a just peace certainly prevailed in the region, in large part because of assumed U.S. influence over Israel.

Even as Egypt and Syria geared up for the 1973 war, their maneuvers were in large part aimed at drawing the United States and the Soviet Union to intervene diplomatically and to pressure Israel to pull out of the territories it had occupied in 1967. That war was a major surprise because Arab armies seemed to have little chance of defeating Israel and recovering all their land. Although the Egyptians and Syrians performed considerably better than most expected, and the Egyptians were able to cross the Suez Canal and recover part of their territories, Israel in the end was able to turn the tide of the war to its advantage.

Politically, however, Egypt and Syria achieved their major objectives in that war, especially in drawing the United States into active diplomacy to resolve the Arab-Israeli issue. There were two reasons why the United States could not simply sit on the sidelines. First, to prevent defeat, Israel needed massive resupply, just as the Egyptians and Syrians needed massive Soviet supplies. Second, there was some chance of a dangerous confrontation with the Soviet Union. Above all, however, was the oil issue. For the first time, the Arab oil-producing states, led by Saudi Arabia, imposed an oil embargo on the United States, demanding that the United States compel Israel to withdraw from the occupied territories. The consequence of that embargo was the quadrupling of oil prices over the following months. Suddenly the United States awoke to a new realization: The Arab-Israeli issue was in fact linked to the issue of oil. This realization led to an axiom in American foreign policy for the past three decades: Arab-Israeli peace is an American interest. Why? Because conflict between Israel and the Arabs makes it difficult to manage the dual American objectives in the region: maintaining the flow of oil to the West at reasonable prices and supporting the security and well-being of the state of Israel.

This axiom in turn defined American diplomacy in the region, from the "shuttle diplomacy" of Secretary of State Henry Kissinger in 1974 and 1975 to the negotiations of the Carter administration that culminated in the Camp David agreements between Israel and Egypt. These efforts resulted in the first peace treaty between Israel and an Arab state and turned the most influential Arab state, Egypt, into an American ally.

In the 1980s, the American diplomatic role was somewhat reduced because the Reagan administration focused its efforts on confronting the Soviet Union instead of on resolving regional issues. But the primary reason for the change in the U.S. role in the region was a change in the strategic environment in the Middle East itself. The Arab world was divided again as Egypt was expelled from the Arab League for making peace with Israel. Israel invaded Lebanon in 1982 in order to expel the Palestine Liberation Organization forces, then found itself trapped in a painful occupation. Most important, Iraq and Iran, the two Persian Gulf powers, were engaged in a major war that lasted from 1980 to 1988, preoccupying them but also endangering and preoccupying their oil-producing neighbors.

As the Reagan era came to an end, Iraq emerged with an aura of political victory after the end of its war with Iran, even though it had suffered hundreds of thousands of casualties and destroyed its own economy. These costs did not prevent President Saddam Hussein from contemplating a new adventure in Kuwait. Simultaneously, Palestinians living in the West Bank and Gaza, lands occupied by Israel in 1967, decided to take matters into their own hands and launched their first major uprising. This Palestinian popular uprising, the *intifada*, captured the news in the Middle East and abroad and revived demands for active diplomatic intervention. The bloodshed during that period generated significant resentment of the United States in the Arab world. In a report I wrote for the chairman of the U.S. House of Representatives Subcommittee on Europe and the Middle East after a visit to several countries in the region in the spring of 1990, I described what I had heard as the highest level of anti-Americanism I had seen in many years. The resentment was high even in countries friendly to the United States, such as Egypt and Jordan.

These perceptions were fueled by an American veto of a UN Security Council resolution on protecting the Palestinians, a congressional resolution declaring Jerusalem to be the united capital of Israel, and massive Soviet Jewish immigration to Israel that many Arabs feared would encourage Israel to keep the West Bank to accommodate the new arrivals. These events were taking place as the Cold War between the Soviet Union and the United States was ending. Most Arabs believed that the end of the Cold War meant the loss of support from the Soviet Union and thus an American-backed Israeli hegemony. The resentment of American policy was pervasive and included many U.S. allies. Even Kuwaiti newspapers called on Arabs "to adopt serious and objective stands against the United States, which persists in a position hostile to the Arab causes."[11] Egyptian President Hosni Mubarak also warned that "the biased U.S. positions will certainly return the region to dependence on the military option."[12]

This environment of resentment was the perfect ground for Saddam Hussein to exploit. Clearly, his aims in invading Kuwait had nothing to do with the Palestinian issue or the Arab-Israeli conflict. But he sought to use the anti-Americanism in the region to his advantage and thus began focusing on the Palestinian-Israeli conflict in the months prior to his invasion. Indeed, when Iraq invaded Kuwait in 1990, Saddam Hussein knew that the United States would try to stop him. What he miscalculated was the willingness of Arab governments to join a military campaign against him in an environment in which public opinion was resentful of America. His miscalculation led not only to his significant defeat and dislodgment from Kuwait but also, as the Cold War ended, to an era of Pax Americana in the Middle East. With the Soviet Union no longer a factor; with new American military bases in the Persian Gulf; and with such key Arab states as Saudi Arabia, Egypt, and even Syria joining the U.S.-led coalition, the Middle East was resigned to a new regional order tailored by U.S. influence. Those who hoped for a strong Arab leader to transform the Arab political order were resigned to their fate with no new hero on the horizon. The rest rallied behind a vision of "a new world order" that would bring benefits to the Middle East through a negotiated settlement of the Arab-Israeli issue, economic prosperity, and the political liberalization that the United States had advocated as the Cold War ended.

Key to this hope were revived American diplomatic efforts, spearheaded by Secretary of State James Baker, that brought Arabs and Israelis together to begin a new negotiating process in Madrid, Spain, in 1991. Peace negotiations were given a further boost in 1993 when the Clinton administration adopted the Oslo Agreements between Israel and the PLO, which envisioned an interim period of autonomy for the Palestinians in the West Bank and Gaza as the two sides negotiated a final peace settlement. Until the very last days of the Clinton administration, that peace process sustained a moderate camp in the Arab world that enabled the containment of radical voices who challenged not only the negotiations but also the American-backed political order.

But when the Palestinian-Israeli negotiations collapsed in July 2000, the paradigm of Pax Americana in the Middle East collapsed with them. As Palestinians and Israelis turned to an escalating cycle of violence in the months that followed, a grim new reality set in. At the end of the decade of American dominance in the Middle East, economic development had never materialized, political reforms had stalled, and the prospect of Arab-Israeli peace had severely diminished. This was the environment that President George W. Bush inherited when he came to office in January 2001.

The attacks of 9/11 raised fundamental new questions about the Middle East and about American policy in the region. But within the region itself, people remained focused on the escalating violence between Israelis and Palestinians. While America saw the Middle East through the haunting prism of the terror attacks on U.S. soil, the Arab world increasingly saw America through the prism of the violent events in its own neighborhood, for which it blamed America as Israel's supporter. What each side saw through these prisms was much uglier than reality.

In the end, it is clear that the regional attitudes toward the United States are primarily shaped by American policies rather than values. In general, Arab resentment goes beyond issues of foreign policy: America is seen as the anchor of a regional order that includes domestic repression and limited economic opportunities. But the surveys show that no issue resonates with more people or does more to shape attitudes toward the United States than the Arab-Israeli dispute. The importance of this issue across the Arab world and in some other parts of the Muslim world needs further explanation, which will be provided in Chapter 4.

Regional Peculiarities

Regardless of the policy issues at the heart of regional anger toward the United States, some attitudes in the Middle East seem hard to explain. Anger with American foreign policy, for example, cannot explain why so many people in the region simply refused to hold bin Laden responsible for the attacks on the United States and thus didn't believe that the war in Afghanistan was justified—even though the Taliban regime was highly unpopular in the Middle East.

A few weeks after the attacks of 9/11, I organized (in cooperation with AMIDEAST)[13] a symposium at the University of Maryland, College Park, which brought together twenty Arab graduate students from a dozen countries on Fulbright scholarships to the United States and twenty American graduate students from the University of Maryland for a discussion of their respective reactions to the attacks. The students found much common ground and also some divergence of views, and by the second day they began to learn more about the intensity of each other's feelings. But one issue stood out: Although all the Arab students strongly condemned the attacks and believed that the perpetrators should be punished, most didn't believe that bin Laden's al-Qaeda was behind them, nor did they even believe that Arabs or Muslims were the likely organizers of the attacks. What explained such a paradoxical outlook?

Indeed, these views were prevalent even outside the Arab world. During a lecture I presented in December 2001 in Baku, Azerbaijan (which had been part of the Soviet Union), none of the 200 students and faculty present said they believed bin Laden was behind the events of 9/11, even as they condemned the attacks. Public opinion surveys conducted in Arab and Muslim countries following 9/11 confirmed this view.

The dialogue at the University of Maryland also revealed three prevailing tendencies in the thinking of the Arab participants:

1. They rejected the possibility that Arabs and Muslims could carry out such atrocities. They were burdened by the thought that someone among them could have been capable of such horror: "Such attacks go against Islamic ideals, therefore Muslims could not have carried them out."

2. There was a tendency to reject the evidence out of hand, in the same way that some African Americans rejected the evidence against O. J. Simpson in the murders of his former wife and her friend: They didn't trust the system, they didn't trust the messenger, and they didn't trust the message. Mistrust of the United States is so widespread, and U.S. power is seen to be so over-

whelming, that the evidence itself is suspected to be fabricated in order to justify American policy.

3. They asked: Who benefited from the attacks? They believed that Arabs and Muslims were losers broadly, and that the Palestinian cause suffered a setback as the United States began seeing the region primarily through the prism of terrorism. The thinking went that Arabs and Muslims would not have inflicted such an outcome on themselves.

This tendency to avoid accountability has become an aspect of the political culture in the Middle East. In part, it is explained by a pervasive narrative of victimization that presents the Arabs, sometimes for good reason, as having been at the mercy of outside powers ever since the end of World War I: quashed aspirations of independence after the war, years of colonial control, Cold War politics, dashed hopes of Arab nationalism, and mostly lost wars with Israel over the past half century. A powerful America with its military presence in the Gulf, its strong support for Israel, and its dominant role in international organizations such as the UN Security Council is a modern symbol of this dependence. This sentiment is held by governments in the region as well as members of the public. During my visits to the Middle East after the Gulf War of 1991, many high-level officials expressed the view that the United States was deliberately keeping Saddam Hussein in place in order to justify the presence of American forces in the region.

Although the intensity of this sense of helpless dependence may be higher in the Arab world than in some other regions, it is also present elsewhere in the world, especially in Latin America, where it has long been a central part of the intellectual culture. There is also a sense of helplessness in relation to the existing authoritarian order that has dominated the lives of people since the emergence of the modern state system in the region. Conspiracy theories are first and foremost a reflection of powerlessness: Those who have no power blame those who are seen to wield it most. Ordinary citizens in much of the region wield little influence in affecting their political system, in transforming their economic prospects, or in influencing the direction of their society broadly, so they blame those they see as powerful.

Governments often benefit from conspiracy theories because these ideas absolve them of responsibility; they are a convenient alternative to accountability. This tendency is ultimately self-defeating because it makes constructive change more difficult. Certainly what happens in the Middle East partly depends on the actions of the outside world. The region's strategic importance means that powerful nations such as the United States will always have a central say in shaping events. Israel, as the most powerful state in the region, also plays a major role in shaping the regional strategic outlook. But rarely does the outcome depend only on one side, even if power is unevenly distributed.

It is important to keep in mind that the habit of disbelieving powerful actors, of being suspicious of their motives, is especially common among the marginal and disenfranchised

segments of society in much of the world. Conspiracy theories are certainly not limited to the Middle East; they are
common in developing nations and elsewhere. We must re-
mind ourselves that they are also common in many marginalized portions of our own society, especially among those who
have never trusted the power of the government. Theories
of conspiracy about the assassination of President John F.
Kennedy have never stopped since his death. Other painful
episodes, such as the Columbine High School shootings and
the Oklahoma City bombing, have generated persistent theories that show distrust of official explanations, usually imag-
ining a mysterious government involvement through such
techniques as "mind control." *The New American*, the maga-
zine of the far-right John Birch Society, has long argued that
there was a Middle East connection to the Oklahoma City
bombing, despite compelling evidence to the contrary.

In fact, many of the conspiracy theories about 9/11 in the
Middle East fed on stories that originated in America. Some
in Arab countries readily quoted a "former American presidential candidate" (Lyndon Larouche) who challenged the
explanation that bin Laden was behind the attacks and suggested looking for the culprit in such areas as "an attempted
military coup d'état against the U.S. government of President George W. Bush," "the current Israeli regime," and the
"Clash of Civilizations policy of Zbigniew Brzezinski, Samuel
Huntington, et al."[14] In comparison, Middle Eastern theories about 9/11 have been less elaborate: From a true story of
the arrest and deportation of possible Israeli spies in the
United States after 9/11, and from the reality that the attack

strengthened U.S.-Israeli relations at the expense of U.S.-Arab relations, some Arabs have constructed an imaginary story about the responsibility of Israel—which to them is all too powerful.

The criticism against the United States as the dominant power and as Israel's backer is further fueled by the fact that most governments in the Middle East often benefit from conspiracy theories that blame others for their failures and because the frustrations of the public are primarily allowed to be channeled verbally. In the end, genuine anger toward American policies is accentuated by verbal assaults in the media as an alternative to actions that might threaten the governments in the region.

Consequences

There is a pervasive resentment of the United States in Arab and Muslim countries, and this resentment is mostly related to American foreign policy. That there is a gap between some core American values and those held by Arabs and Muslims, but also some overlap, should not be surprising. Viewing the gap through a global perspective that highlights a similar discrepancy between the United States and other countries around the world should reduce the puzzlement. Certainly the intensity of resentment of the United States among Arabs and Muslims is higher than that in other regions. But in the end the question is about consequences: Is this gap, or the intensity of public anger toward the United

States, dangerous for American interests? Does it in any way affect the American war on terrorism?

Indeed, if one regards al-Qaeda as a special case that requires its own explanation, resentment of the United States in the Middle East and in other Muslim countries has not historically translated into anti-American terrorism. Except for al-Qaeda, the Middle East has not led other parts of the world in terrorist attacks against American targets. It is thus reasonable to ask whether public opinion in the region is seriously detrimental to American foreign policy, especially given that most states in the Middle East are authoritarian and thus seemingly capable of disregarding the wishes of their publics. Does public opinion matter in the Middle East, or can it be completely disregarded in the shaping of American foreign policy? These important questions are the subject of the next chapter.

3

Does Public Opinion in the Middle East Matter?

When Egypt and Israel came together at Camp David, Maryland, in September 1978 to negotiate the terms of their peace agreement, an early confrontation between Menachem Begin, Israel's prime minister, and Egyptian President Anwar Sadat led U.S. President Jimmy Carter to separate them from each other for much of the negotiations. The confrontation was in part over the extent to which Sadat could influence Egyptian public sentiment in making compromises in the negotiations. As President Carter recalled, Begin argued that "the people of Egypt could be easily manipulated by Sadat, and their beliefs and attitudes could be shaped by their leader."[1] As an example, Begin cited Sadat's ability to convince his people that the Soviets were their best friends, only to later cast them as Egypt's worst enemy. Sadat's reaction was predictable anger.

The view expressed by Menachem Begin—that authoritarian governments in the region are always able to shape public opinion, or at least to resist it when necessary, regardless of how intense public anger is—has gained many adherents in the United States since the 1991 Gulf War. When Arab governments succeeded in overcoming apparent public opposition to a war with Iraq by joining the American-led coalition, the notion that Arab public opinion is an important consideration in forming public policy was significantly weakened. Testifying before the Senate Foreign Relations Committee on July 31, 2002, about the prospects of war with Iraq, a Middle East analyst, Fouad Ajami, suggested that the United States should leave the issue of Arab public opinion to Arab governments, adding that "they don't know how to develop their populations . . . but they know how to stay in power—that's what the game is all about."[2]

In many ways there is truth to the proposition that Arab governments have been very good at simply surviving. The record is impressive: In Egypt, the government that has ruled over the country since the overthrow of the monarchy in 1952 remains in place despite decades of upheavals—war in 1956, a devastating defeat in 1967, a war of attrition with Israel in 1969–1970, and another major war in 1973. Politically, the Egyptian government has taken its people from an alliance with the Soviet Union to an alliance with the United States. Regionally, Egypt went from the champion of the pan-Arab movement and the Palestinian cause to becoming the first Arab country to make peace with Israel and be expelled from the Arab League. Throughout many of these years, Egypt's economic prospects have been bleak. It is the sort of volatile mixture that leads scholars to expect continued political instability, but the government is still in place with no apparent threat to its survival.

Similarly, the Hashemite monarchy in Jordan has ruled over the country since its inception under British mandate in 1920, even though the family originated in the Hijaz in Saudi Arabia. A small, poor nation surrounded by more powerful neighbors, including Iraq, Syria, Israel, and Saudi Arabia, Jordan took the brunt of the burden of the Palestinian refugee problem after the 1948 and 1967 wars. It lost control of the West Bank to Israel in war and faced what amounted to a mini–civil war with the Palestinians in 1970. Its economy dropped significantly after the 1991 Gulf War. During that war, it failed to join the American-led coalition, even though it had been one of America's closest friends in the Middle East. Its public continually expresses a high degree of anger with American foreign policy, especially with the events in Palestine, across the Jordan River. Yet the Hashemite monarchy remains, and its official relations with America are as friendly as ever.

This story of government continuity repeats itself in places such as Morocco and Tunisia and even Libya, where Muammar al-Qaddafi has been in power since 1969. In Syria, the secular Arab nationalist government of the Baath party has been in place since the mid-1960s. In the Arab Gulf, every government that emerged at the founding of the states remains in power. In Iraq, the Baathist government that ruled the state from the mid-1960s until the collapse of Saddam Hussein survived extraordinary disasters, including an eight-year war with Iran that resulted in hundreds of thousands of Iraqi casualties and took the country from wealth to near bankruptcy. It survived a defeat by the American-led coalition in 1991, which cost many more lives and further economic devastation, and it survived a decade of the most stringent economic sanctions ever imposed by the international community. This remarkable record explains why many analysts suggest a strategy toward the Middle East that ignores public sentiments and focuses on providing incentives and threats to governments while allowing these regimes to worry about their own survival.

This is a mistake. Certainly one has to deal with governments above all, since states remain the primary players in international politics. But there are important reasons why public opinion cannot be ignored. First, it has never been the case, even in the era of limited information, that public opinion in the Middle East had no effect on the policies of states, as all governments are in part concerned with maintaining their popular legitimacy. Second, in the past decade the globalization of information technology has taken away much of the governments' monopoly over an important instrument of control that was previously at their disposal. Third, as was horribly demonstrated by the terrorist attacks against the United States, the threat of terrorism emanates above all from nonstate actors. The capacity of disaffected individuals and groups to inflict pain on states has dramatically increased in an era when states have decreased capacity to control the flow of weapons technology and information. Whether or not states can suppress opposition, which increases public anger even more, and contain terrorism at the same time is less certain than in the past.

The Legitimacy Factor

Despite the record of stability of authoritarian governments in the region, there have also been marked episodes of consequential public opposition. Whatever the logic of Menachem Begin's argument that President Sadat should ignore his public, the Egyptian leader ultimately paid with his life for his courage. Although revolutions are scarce in history, and certainly have been scarce in the Middle East, they do occur, and often unpredictably. The pro-American shah of Iran, who seemingly succeeded in establishing a robust state with effective and ruthless security services, was overthrown by a clergy-led popular revolution in 1979—a revolution that had significant consequences for Iran's foreign policy, regional politics, and American interests. The fact that America's ally in the region, King Hussein of Jordan, found himself opposing the American-led coalition against Iraq in 1991 was a function of his assessment that he would not otherwise be able to overcome the anger of his public. Certainly, governments in the region have been more successful at survival in recent years. But a period of upheaval and instability in the region following the Suez crisis of 1956 led to the overthrow of the pro-Western monarchy in Iraq; the emergence of a Baathist, Arab-nationalist regime in Syria; and significant threats to pro-Western governments in the region, especially in Lebanon and Jordan. Since then governments have succeeded in consolidating their power, both by creating stronger state identities and by establishing effective security services that have become the governments' first line of defense. It is clear, therefore, that when governments in the region go against the wishes of their publics, they can succeed only to the extent that they can employ effective coercive means.

The ability of governments in the region to overcome public dissent through effective state security apparatuses is at the heart of the logic of those who have confidence that these states can ignore the wishes of their people. But even in the days when many states had near monopolies on information, the extent to which the public accepted the government's legitimacy was always a factor in official calculations. This notion of legitimacy is central: In America we take it for granted that our government is legitimate because our electoral system bestows legitimacy upon our elected representatives. Even when presidents receive low approval ratings, most Americans do not question their legitimacy until their terms expire. Popularity is important, but legitimacy is even more central. Because there is an absence of electoral legitimacy in much of the Middle East, it is harder to distinguish between popularity and legitimacy. Governments are legitimate to the extent that they are seen as serving the causes that their people support.

This issue of legitimacy complicates the exercise of coercive power by governments in two ways. First, the more illegitimate a government feels, the more repressive resources it has to employ. It is like swimming against a rapid tide. This strategy stresses a government's available resources and creates uncertainty about the point at which the members of the state security apparatus, who are after all also members of society, will begin to empathize more with the public than with the government. In 1979, for example, a key reason for the success of the Iranian revolution was that portions of the military, especially the air force cadets, joined the revolution and confronted other branches of the military. Legitimacy allows a more efficient use of resources that enhances a government's ability to maintain power.

Second, legitimacy provides a protective cushion in times of crisis by buying governments time when there is a temporary reduction in their coercive capabilities. A good case in point was Egyptian President Nasser's ability to survive the devastating defeat by Israel in 1967. As Israeli jet fighters flew freely over Cairo, Nasser resigned his presidency, possibly as a tactical move. Within hours millions of Egyptians took to the street to ask him to reverse his resignation. Governments in the Middle East, like others, are driven above all by the need to survive, so they maintain significant coercive capabilities. But none can afford to ignore the question of legitimacy.

When America pursues a strategy that ignores public sentiments in the region, we should have no illusion about the means that governments will have to employ to accommodate such policies: more repression. Indeed, during the Gulf War of 1991, we found that governments such as Jordan that had responded to our earlier calls for political democratization, and that thus had to be more responsive to public opinion, were inclined to oppose U.S. policies, and those who supported U.S. policies were inclined to become more repressive in order to maintain that unpopular course.

The Impact of the Information Revolution

Still, we must never underestimate the resources that have been available to states in the region to overcome public dissent. One of those resources has been control of information, which has helped governments shape public opinion as well as contain it. One way to reduce concerns about public opinion is to help shape it, and governments in the region have long held significant abilities to mold public perceptions and expectations in a manner that reduced the threat of opposition.

Even in the middle of the twentieth century, information was used by governments to affect politics across the borders of Arab states as well. Long before the information revolution that took place in the 1990s, information was employed by governments and subnational groups to advance their causes. In the 1950s and 1960s, Egypt employed effective radio programs, especially *Sawt al-Arab* (The Voice of Arabs), to spread its pan-Arabist message

across the region and to undermine conservative governments, while its adversaries constantly attempted to jam
these broadcasts. Israel produced radio programs in popular Egyptian dialect, using Israeli Jews of Egyptian descent,
to undermine Egypt's government in the 1960s. In the
1970s, the Islamic revolutionaries in Iran used recorded
cassettes to spread the message of their leader, the Ayatullah Ruhollah Khomeini, among the Iranian public despite
the state monopoly over the media. Britain, France, and
the United States have had radio reach in much of the region, including programs in Arabic, but none of these programs came close to the reach and diversity of the media
available to Arab consumers today. Never have governments been less able to control the flow of information to
their public than in recent years.

The 1991 Gulf War ushered in the CNN phenomenon: instant media coverage on a global scale. The 2001 attacks on
the United States ushered in the era of al-Jazeera, a Qatari-
based satellite television station that can be seen throughout
the Arab world and in many other regions. In a decade a true
revolution took place in the arena of information, with a
rapid drop in the cost of satellite dishes and their proliferation in the region, technological advances in print media that
allowed simultaneous printing of newspapers in many parts
of the world, and the emergence of private entrepreneurs
who sought to exploit these phenomena to start their own
media enterprises for both glory and profit. This revolution
has significantly undermined the ability of governments to
control the information flow to their own societies, even

though most media outlets in the Middle East have remained under the control of governments.

It is important to understand the nature of this phenomenon and why it has posed such a challenge to governments in the Arab world. Surveys show that al-Jazeera is more watched across Arab boundaries than other stations, and in places such as Saudi Arabia it even supersedes the news viewership of Saudi channels, but it is by no means alone. In fact, the success of al-Jazeera is a product of the extraordinary choices that Arabs have when they turn on their televisions or tune in to their radio stations. This choice ultimately forces the media to be more consumer-conscious.

In the American discussion of the role of al-Jazeera and other media, the focus has been on what has been seen as decided editorial bias by the station and its commentators that fuels anti-American sentiments. There was evidence that those who watched the station's programs had somewhat more unfavorable impressions of America than others. There was the inescapable fact that this outlet had aired bin Laden's speeches, invited his sympathizers to debate his opponents, and hosted representatives of the Taliban regime. It highlighted the civilian casualties among Muslims in Afghanistan much more than American television did, and many of its guests and callers from around the Arab world have expressed harsh criticism of the United States, especially during periods of violence in the Palestinian areas. The apparent bias has resulted in complaints by the U.S. government, despite its calls for freer media in the Middle East, and in requests from the Qatari government that the station change its tone. This dilemma—on the one hand encouraging free press while on the other hand asking governments to curb media freedom—was well summarized by Ambassador Christopher Ross, one of the few American diplomats who is fluent in Arabic, who appeared on al-Jazeera to defend the administration's position: "You at al-Jazeera know that since al-Jazeera's inception, the U.S. administration has been a great admirer of the channel. It is true, however, that during a specific time, some American officials expressed their concerns that al-Jazeera was broadcasting announcements made by al-Qaeda organization officials on a regular basis. The U.S. government considered that to be a message inciting violence."[3]

It is true that al-Jazeera, like most media outlets, probably has an editorial agenda; that its staff, like those of most media sources, is of varying professional quality; and that in times of pain and tragedy some of its reporters find it hard to separate reporting from commentary. However, in general it has done a far better job than most outlets in the region, and better than some elsewhere in the world. The real issue is the extent to which its editorial policy or coverage is responsible for the attitudes of the Arab public on issues related to foreign policy. There is a misconception of what the al-Jazeera phenomenon represents: It reflects public opinion much more than it shapes it. It succeeds in large part because it is responsive to public attitudes. This is a new era in Middle East broadcasting.

In the days when governments had a near monopoly on the media within their boundaries, they had a captive audience. Their aim was very clear: to project a picture that helped the government stay in power. The media were a significant instrument of policy available to the rulers. As such, it was not uncommon for a good portion of the news, even the top of the news, to be dedicated to showing a ruler individually greeting every single one of dozens of dignitaries, often with nothing more than background music. Regardless of what the public wanted to see, no ruler wanted to offend a single important local leader by leaving him out of the picture.

Today some such broadcasts remain, but few people, except perhaps those dignitaries and their families, watch them because the public has choices. The proliferation of media outlets, both governmental and private, and the increasing public access to these outlets have changed the nature of broadcasting strategy. It is now about securing the largest market share in the Arab world. Successful media outlets in the Middle East prevail largely because they understand the logic of the new consumer market. Stations such as the Middle East Broadcasting Corporation (MBC) and al-Jazeera have been innovative in attempting to understand what the Arab consumer is looking for. Abu Dhabi TV, which has attempted to compete with these outlets, revamped its programming after commissioning substantial consumer surveys. In short, the Arab public, like viewers who have choices elsewhere, turns to the stations that provide the product they most like and whose views and style resonate the most. When these stations fail to deliver, consumers will turn elsewhere. It is the logic of the market.

The size of the market itself has significantly changed in the Arab world over the past decade. With new technological progress, especially satellites, a station out of a small country such as Qatar can now reach everywhere. Many stations simultaneously broadcast through the World Wide Web. This phenomenon has redefined the "consumer" for these media. Whereas in the past, most government-controlled media were concerned above all with their own local market in their own Arab country in order to enhance the state's identity and bolster the power of the government, the new media see the entire Arab world as their potential market. The market in this case is defined by language: Every Arabic-speaking person, regardless of where he or she lives, is a potential consumer. Thus, the consumer for competitive media outlets is no longer the Qatari, the Egyptian, the Jordanian, or the Saudi as such. It is now "the Arab." Therefore, in order to reach the largest market segment, a successful outlet must appeal to the largest number of Arabs across state borders. To do so, the outlet must focus on the issues that many Arabs have in common and that resonate with the largest portion of the Arab public. Such issues are often matters of collective identity and foreign policy, especially the Arab-Israeli conflict.

It is necessary to put this responsiveness of successful media in historical perspective. Al-Jazeera has been widely criticized for being more anti-Israel than other stations. After 9/11 it was also criticized for being anti-American. Yet in the late 1990s, when the Palestinian negotiations seemed to be moving forward and many thought peace to be inevitable, al-Jazeera was the first Arab media outlet to invite Israeli representatives to appear regularly on its programs. It was the first to have a reporter covering the Israeli parliament, the Knesset, to convey the workings of the Israeli system to many homes around the Arab world, from Morocco to Saudi Arabia, that had rarely seen a real picture of Israel or Israeli politics. At the time, critics in the Arab world accused it of "normalizing" Israel for its audience and of being a Zionist agent serving Israeli interests.

Al-Jazeera's change in tone after the collapse of the Camp David peace negotiations in July 2000 and the subsequent escalation in Palestinian-Israeli violence reflected the change in the public mood. It certainly wasn't the maker of the public mood. Had al-Jazeera stuck to the tone it had taken before, its competitors would have quickly filled the gap. It has continued to be criticized in the United States and also has significant critics among Arab governments who felt threatened by its kind of reporting. It has often broken taboos by inviting opposition figures to debate government supporters from many Arab states, including Morocco, Egypt, and Saudi Arabia. It has irritated these governments to the point of straining relations between a number of Arab countries and the Qatari government, which has been held responsible for al-Jazeera's broadcasts, and al-Jazeera's offices in other Arab capitals have often been shut down. These reactions are a reminder that although states feel threatened by the new phenomenon, they still have important methods of dealing with it. This relationship between the globalization of information that undermines the power of governments and the levers that governments still press to mitigate its impact will be central in the future of the media in the region.

The New Media and the Role of the State

In the past, Arab governments have been able to limit the emotions of their publics by limiting their people's exposure to painful pictures. During the Gulf War of 1991, the Arab states that joined the American-led coalition cooperated with the United States in an information campaign that was specifically designed to limit the reach of Saddam Hussein's story and to restrict coverage of issues that could have increased public anger. Today the public often watches live images of death and injury of Palestinian civilians, footage of Israeli tanks in West Bank cities, and emotional interviews with parents of fallen children. They feel helpless and humiliated but also angry at the apparent impotence of their governments. In some instances, callers specifically criticize Arab governments, call them agents of America or Zionism, and exhort the public to surround the security forces in their own countries to embarrass them for their inability to help the Palestinians. These broadcasts have no doubt been instrumental in mobilizing the large demonstrations that took place during the worst months of the Israeli campaign against Palestinian cities in the spring of 2002.

These broadcasts, especially during times of high public passions, make governments in the region feel insecure, and

Pax Americana in the Middle East: 1991–1998 (by Shibley Telhami; illustration by Paul Duginski. Originally appeared in the *Los Angeles Times* on February 15, 1998)

when their legitimacy is brought into question, they often take action. In a program on al-Jazeera television in August 2002, an Arab American professor accused Jordan of having a pro-Israeli stance even before it signed a peace treaty with Israel in 1994. He also claimed that King Hussein, who died of cancer in 1999, had cooperated with the U.S. intelligence apparatus. The Jordanian government reacted by closing al-Jazeera's office in Amman, arguing that al-Jazeera "continuously intends to harm Jordan and its national stands whether directly or indirectly.",

Only days before, relations between Saudi Arabia and Qatar had plunged to a new low after al-Jazeera aired the views of Saudi dissidents who blasted the royal family and Saudi officials accused the station of serving Zionist interests and aiming to sow discord among Arabs. These significant political pressures from many quarters of the Arab world as well as from the United States may have had an occasional impact, but on the whole al-Jazeera has maintained its open style. The question is whether the power of states will be so great that new limitations will be imposed on the regional media despite the market demand for open news.

Even in the midst of this new media phenomenon, states are still significant players. In places such as Egypt, where most people still do not have access to satellite television, the government's own TV stations dominate. Even stations that are set up as "private" enterprises have governmental links. MBC television is owned by members of the royal family in Saudi Arabia. Al-Jazeera is theoretically modeled after the British Broadcasting Corporation (BBC), as a publicly subsidized station. The original logic was that once it succeeded in gaining a significant market share in the Arab world, its advertising revenue would be sufficient to sustain the station. It would then go completely private five years after its inception. This logic had a central flaw: Governments in the region had much say in advertising revenue. As al-Jazeera became more and more influential and therefore more and more attractive as an advertising venue, the very style that made it so popular also made it threatening to governments. Big corporations that command the biggest advertising budgets typically do their business with governments or businesses that are associated with the state. When a large company doing business in Saudi Arabia or Egypt senses tension between those governments and al-Jazeera, they are unlikely to alienate their patron governments by helping to subsidize the Qatari station. For these reasons, al-Jazeera has been unable to reap the benefits of its popularity in a manner that would ensure its independence.

The Qatari government has the power to simply shut al-Jazeera down overnight. The question is, why doesn't it? And how is Qatar, a small nation dwarfed by mightier neighbors, able to resist constant pressure from more powerful Arab countries? It is clear that the Qataris have used al-Jazeera to turn a media tide that went against them in the early and middle 1990s. A state whose relations with its bigger neighbor Saudi Arabia have often lacked warmth, Qatar was frequently the subject of criticism in the Saudi-dominated pan-Arab media. Indeed, the 1980s in the Arab world were characterized by the rise of Saudi investment in influential media outlets, including important newspapers that were distributed in much of the Arab world. These media often criticized the Qataris, especially in the mid-1990s, when Qatar initiated a dialogue with Israel during a low point in the peace process. By backing an innovative and influential television station, the Qataris have managed to control an outlet that the Saudis and others fear and to reduce the influence of the Saudi-backed media. In that sense, al-Jazeera has been an asset for the Qatari government.

Ultimately, however, one has to consider the source of Qatari confidence in resisting such mighty political pressures from other Arab states. The answer is simple: hosting American military bases. The strategic relationship that Qatar has developed with the United States, especially at a time when the Saudis were reluctant to allow American bases in the kingdom during a possible war on Iraq, has given the Qataris a protective cushion that allows them to withstand criticism from other friends of the United States in the region. In fact, even as many in the United States were criticizing al-Jazeera for anti-American bias, and sometimes for sympathizing with Iraq, Qatar's ruler decided to allow enlargement of American bases to replicate some of the installations in Saudi Arabia.

When the United States launched attacks against Arab targets in Iraq from Qatari bases, al-Jazeera faced a dilemma. Its response was to highlight the American role, speaking of the United States as the "occupying force," while downplaying the Qatari role.

All this is to say that governments are still central players, even in the era of information revolution. But the phenomenon does pose major challenges to governments if only by enabling other governments, even small hostile ones, to reach a broad public. Radio stations broadcasting from outside the Middle East, especially from Europe, and the increasing use of the Internet have undermined the governments' monopoly over information. If al-Jazeera gives up its open style and stops catering to consumer taste, market demand will be met by another aspiring station.

For this reason, Arab governments, which still hold significant capacity to contain dissent, are considerably less certain today about the consequences of crises that inflame public passions. They are swimming in uncharted waters.

Globalization and Public Empowerment

On September 10, 2001, I delivered a speech in Washington, D.C., before the National Council on U.S.-Arab Relations in which I expressed my greatest fear: that the empowering message of suicide bombings in an environment of sustained humiliation and despair means that this horrible method could soon be employed outside the Arab-Israeli arena by ruthless terrorists exploiting that environment. I certainly had no idea how close to home such a threat hovered.

The impact of the borderless flow of information on the media is only one of the changes that has reduced governments' confidence in their usual ability to resist public displeasure. As governments learn from previous threats how to improve their capacity to confront the next threat, the individuals and groups opposed to them also learn. One aspect of the information revolution has been easier access to technology and easier coordination among individuals and groups that are geographically separated. The *New York Times* columnist Thomas Friedman put it this way:

The third balance that you have to pay attention to in the globalization system—the one that is really the newest of all—is the balance between individuals and nation-states. Because globalization has brought down many of the walls that limited the movement and reach of people, and because it has simultaneously wired the world into networks, it gives more power to individuals to influence both markets and nation-states than at any time in history. So you have today not only a superpower . . . you have Super-empowered individuals. Some of these Super-empowered individuals are quite angry, some of them quite wonderful—but all of them are now able to act directly on the world stage without the traditional mediation of governments, corporations or any other public or private institutions.[5]

Although states have by no means lost their centrality, and although most will likely find new ways to deal with the challenges posed by globalization, there is little doubt that they now face new challenges and thus have doubts about the effectiveness of old instruments of policy. They are less confident about their abilities as they assess the nature of the threats against them. Some are more vulnerable than others. In the Middle East, governments generally face the following dilemma: In order to accommodate the challenges of globalization, they must open up the political and economic system; but in order to resist increasing public pressure in the short term, they are inclined to employ repressive measures that further close the system. Either way, the risks are high.

What is also clear is that publics see in the new opportunities new sources of inspiration that are not linked to governments and states. Historically, the frustrated Arab public has pinned its hope for change on some outside government or some other outside actor. In 1990, those who were again frustrated by Israeli actions and by a sense of weakness after the end of the Cold War pinned their aspirations on the prospects of powerful leaders such as Saddam Hussein. Even though many in the region disliked him for his ruthlessness and for his war with Iran, the prospect of a powerful Arab state that could stand up to foreign power was appealing. When Saddam lost the Gulf War, the hopes of those banking on him were dashed. In the 1960s, those who opposed "Western imperialism" or sought to "liberate Palestine," or even to change their own governments, pinned their hopes on regional leaders such as Gamal Abdel Nasser of Egypt. When he failed to deliver military victory in 1967 and instead lost some of his own territories to Israel, there was a massive sense of resignation and loss of hope across the region. This sense was exploited shortly afterward by the Palestinian guerrilla groups trying to inspire support outside the state, since most in the region had lost hope that governments could deliver. To inspire hope, these groups turned a tactical victory into a strategic advantage of mythic proportion.

That tactical victory was the Battle of Karameh in Jordan in March 1968. Coming on the heels of the 1967 Arab defeat, which resulted in Israeli control of the rest of Palestine and in a new wave of refugees, the Battle of Karameh became an instant legend of the Palestinian movement. Although many of the details are disputed, the battle involved about 1,500 Israeli soldiers raiding Palestinian guerrilla bases in the town of Karameh, where approximately 300 Palestinian commandos were stationed. The Palestinians engaged the Israeli forces in a bloody battle that resulted in the deaths of twenty-eight Israelis and the wounding of ninety. But word quickly spread of Palestinian heroics with claims of much bigger Israeli losses, comparing the relative success of the PLO to the collective failure of Arab states in the 1967 war. Karameh, which means "dignity" in Arabic, became a metaphor for Palestinian self-reliance and a source of regional inspiration. Within twenty-four hours, 5,000 volunteers applied to join the forces of the Palestinian group Fatah.

Although this new form of inspiration was linked to nonstate actors, the groups themselves were the source of inspiration; regional hope was focused on *supporting* them, not on *emulating* their action. Today, few people believe that governments and leaders in the region will be able to deliver. As the media convey pictures of mounting Palestinian casualties and their own economic and political prospects remain limited, their contempt for governments has been growing. Their new inspiration for violent change is a form of the power of individuals and nonstate groups, and their new heroes are Lebanese guerrillas and the Palestinians of the *intifada*. Horrible as they are, suicide bombings are empowering to many as a method that overcomes great odds and redefines the distribution of power. More importantly, these methods can be easily emulated because the resources and organization required to carry them out are minimal. Given the relative ease of obtaining weapons and information on how to build them, and significantly enhanced coordination capabilities across space and geographic boundaries, the threat is real. It is not hard to imagine that ambitious and ruthless individuals and groups will increasingly be able to recruit members among the desperate to challenge the states.

In the next phase, the suicide-bombing phenomenon may aim at Arab state institutions as well as increasing numbers of foreign targets. The lethality of such attacks is likely to increase as states deploy significant resources to prevent them. Most states are likely to win in the end, as they have proven to be resilient in the face of change. But few governments want to take the risk. If they succeed in overcoming the mounting challenge, it will be through repressive measures, especially in the short term.

Despite mounting domestic challenges to their stability, Arab governments still hold more power domestically than they do internationally. Though their public may want them to take a more defiant position toward the United States, or a more confrontational position toward Israel, they still have greater capacity to resist their public than to accommodate its wishes. Militarily, Arab governments do not have significant options in relation to Israel. One of the outcomes of the peace agreement between Egypt and Israel has been that Arab states no longer have serious military capability for fighting a conventional war with Israel. Furthermore, many of them have a strong interest in maintaining strategic relations with the United States. Egypt, for example, receives $2 billion a year in U.S. aid, second only to the $3 billion Israel receives. And its military is supplied by, and strongly tied to, the U.S. military. Jordan, which is a vulnerable state with insignificant military capabilities, needs Washington's continued backing.

But mounting pressure has had some impact on these states' foreign policies, leading Egypt to reduce its contacts with Israel and inducing Jordan to consider the same action in response to the Palestinian-Israeli crisis in the spring of 2002. With every new escalation in the conflict, public pressure demands new reactions. This increasing tension between domestic and foreign policies forces governments to constantly reassess their options.

War initiated by Arab states is unlikely, as Arab governments would stand to lose more than they stand to gain. But there is an absence of equilibrium in regional politics at the outset of the twenty-first century that is likely to lead to unanticipated consequences, even if those consequences may not be a conventional Arab-Israeli war: On the one hand, many Arab governments need strong relations with the United States and do not wish for confrontation with Israel; on the other hand, this position exacerbates the anger of an increasingly restless Arab public. Assessments of likely outcomes cannot be limited to pure calculations about the distribution of military power but must include the degree of public and government motivation. In 1973, the entire international community, including Israel and the United States, failed to anticipate the war by Syria and Egypt to regain their lost territories for a simple reason: It seemed entirely irrational to expect states to wage wars they knew they had little chance of winning. Former Secretary of State Henry Kissinger later explained that he had to modify his outlook on Middle Eastern politics following that war. "Our definition of rationality did not take seriously the notion of starting an unwinnable war to restore self-respect," he wrote.[6]

At the outset of the twenty-first century, there is a pervasive sense of humiliation and loss of self-respect and a desperate desire to restore dignity across the Middle East, the consequences of which are especially unpredictable in the uncharted waters of the era of globalization. Some of this despair is connected to political and economic systems that have not served their populations well. The Arab population is considerably younger than the global average. Arab unemployment rates were over 20 percent in 2000 in several states, the highest being in the devastated Palestinian areas, where it reached 40 percent in 2000 while still growing. A report released by the UN Development Programme about human development in Arab states was critical of political and economic conditions in the region. Although the region had made progress in many areas since 1970, including substantially increasing life expectancy and doubling the literacy rate (tripling it for women), more than half of Arab women still remained illiterate. More critically, the report concluded that the region had the lowest (out of seven world regions: North America, Oceania, Europe, Latin America and the Caribbean, South and East Asia, Sub-Saharan Africa, and

Arab Countries) "freedom score," which measures a broad range of political and civil rights and freedoms enjoyed in reality rather than in declared documents and policies. The combined gross domestic product (GDP) of all twenty-two members of the Arab League stood at $531.2 billion in 1999—less than that of a single European country, Spain ($595.5 billion).

These political and economic sources for public anger are real, but they are exacerbated by the Arab-Israeli issue, which remains a central source of a collective psychology of humiliation in the Arab world. Explaining the reasons is the aim of the next chapter.

4

The Role of the
Arab–Israeli Issue

And to America, I say to it and to its people this:
I swear by God the Great, America will never dream
and those who live in America will never taste security and safety unless we feel security and safety in
our land and in Palestine.

—Usama bin Laden, October 7, 2001

As American attacks commenced on al-Qaeda and its hosts,
the Taliban regime in Afghanistan, Usama bin Laden ended
a speech intended to rally Arab and Muslim support by suggesting that his terrorism was motivated by the pain in Palestine. Yet it is clear from what al-Qaeda has stood for historically, from bin Laden's own record, that Palestine has not
been a priority for his organization. Moreover, al-Qaeda and

many Islamists around the world viewed the nationalist Palestine Liberation Organization, and the Palestinian national movement in general, with disdain, for they themselves sought a borderless Islamist world, not a secularized divided one. According to some of those who knew al-Qaeda's inner workings and who have cooperated with U.S. investigators since the fall of 2001, al-Qaeda viewed even the Islamist Palestinian group Hamas with suspicion as a nationalist group focused on Palestine only, which had never sent fighters on behalf of other Muslim causes in places such as Chechnya, Bosnia, or Afghanistan. The question is: Why did bin Laden invoke the Palestinian issue in his hour of desperate need for support? The answer is simple: No other issue resonates with the public in the Arab world, and many other parts of the Muslim world, more deeply than Palestine. No other issue shapes the regional perceptions of America more fundamentally than the issue of Palestine.

Ever since the creation of the state of Israel, Arab governments have often used the Palestinian issue for their own political ends, sometimes to mask internal problems. When Iraq invaded Kuwait for reasons that obviously had nothing to do with Palestine or Israel, its leaders focused their rhetoric primarily on these issues, portraying themselves as champions of the Palestinian cause. After the Gulf War commenced in 1991, Iraq quickly fired missiles at Israel in an attempt to turn the war into an Arab-Israeli conflict. And when Saddam Hussein worried about new American war plans to dislodge his government in August 2002, his speech to begin preparing the Iraqi people and others in the Arab world saluted "the Arabs in the forefront of whom come the heroic people of Palestine, and . . . every honorable warrior of the faithful who met his God with a pure heart."[1] Given that the motives of many Arab governments often have little to do with Palestine, why, one has to ask, do they mention this issue so often?

When the Bush administration came to office in early 2001, the prospects of Palestinian-Israeli peace were small, which is one reason that the administration was reluctant to make the issue a priority in its agenda. U.S. officials also assumed that, the human tragedy aside, the continuing violence was unlikely to seriously affect vital American interests, especially in the Gulf region. They saw Arab governments such as Saudi Arabia as paying lip service to the Palestinian issue, but no one believed they would allow this matter to affect their policies or undermine their relations with the United States.

The administration faced a surprising challenge to this view in the spring of 2001, months before the horror of 9/11. Crown Prince Abdullah of Saudi Arabia, who was in effect running the country, turned down President Bush's invitation to visit the White House because of his displeasure with American foreign policy regarding Palestine. According to many accounts, this act puzzled the president more than any other event in the Middle East and led to reassessment of his administration's policy.

Regardless of the real motives of governments in the region, which are, like governments elsewhere, primarily driven by calculations of survival, the very fact that most appeal to the question of Palestine indicates that they know the cause resonates with their publics. In crisis situations, when government legitimacy is often challenged, the appeal to this particular issue resonates the most, and Arab leaders of many nationalities often rush to wrap themselves in Palestinian flags.

The Evidence

The Saudi and other Arab governments have increasingly learned the depth of the public anger in their countries over the Palestinian issue. In surveys I commissioned in March 2001 in five Arab states—Saudi Arabia, the United Arab Emirates, Kuwait, Lebanon, and Egypt—public attitudes on this question were decidedly clear. In the first four countries, about 60 percent of the respondents identified the Palestinian conflict as the "single most important issue" to them personally, while about 20 percent more said it was among their top three issues. In Egypt, 79 percent identified it as "the single most important issue." Similar results were attained in a ten-nation Zogby International survey[2] in spring 2002 that included five Arab countries, three other Muslim countries, Venezuela, and France. In all Arab countries surveyed, roughly two-thirds of the respondents said that the Palestinian issue is "the most important" or a "very important" issue facing the Arab world today. Roughly the same percentage in two of the non-Arab Muslim states, Pakistan and Indonesia, agreed with the Arab respondents. Though these polls do not mean that Palestine is more important than jobs or putting food on the table, they clearly indicate the depth of feeling on the matter in these countries.

Contrary to the notion that these attitudes were driven by the phenomenon of al-Jazeera and other new media, there was no evidence in the survey to support such a theory. In fact, there was no clear difference between the depth of feelings on Palestine between those who watched al-Jazeera and those who didn't in three of the countries studied, and the results in Egypt and Saudi Arabia went against conventional wisdom: In those countries, those who watched al-Jazeera tended to be somewhat less passionate about Palestine than those who did not.

Not only did the Arab public rank the Palestinian issue high in its priorities, but it clearly formed its attitudes toward the United States on the basis of this issue. In a survey I conducted in February 2002 of Saudi elites—defined as media professionals, academics, and Chamber of Commerce members—43 percent said their frustrations with the United States would be completely removed, and 23 percent said they would be significantly reduced, if America brokered a just and lasting peace in the Arab-Israeli conflict. These results were supported by findings in the Zogby survey in April 2002, in which the overwhelming majorities in all Arab and Muslim states, except Iran, said they would have a more favorable view of the United States if it "were to apply pressure to assure the creation of a Palestinian state."

Other surveys, including polls by Gallup, also show the importance of this issue among the public in the region, confirming the view that many analysts, scholars, and journalists have long recognized based on interviews and conversations with people in the region. However, it is not clear why this issue remains so important to Arabs and Muslims, including many who are far away from the Israeli-Palestinian arena. This importance requires explanation.

Why the Palestinian Issue Is Important

There is reason to doubt the degree to which Arabs truly care about the Palestinian issue, given the behavior of many Arab governments in the past and the apparent negative attitudes toward Palestinians by parts of the Arab public in countries such as Lebanon, Kuwait, and Jordan. Palestinian refugees have suffered in most of their host countries, especially Lebanon, and have been granted citizenship only in Jordan. After the liberation of Kuwait in 1991, that country's government expelled most Palestinians in its territories because the Palestinian leadership had sympathized with Iraq. The outcome of the Gulf War of 1991 also worsened relations between most Gulf Arab countries and the PLO. In fact, to many it seemed that the Gulf War had significantly, seemingly irreversibly, reduced the importance of the Palestinian issue in Arab politics.

This conclusion is a misreading of history. The Palestinian issue is not about liking or disliking Yasser Arafat, believing in the Palestinian national movement as such, or even being especially fond of individual Palestinians. It is an issue of *identity*. Its role in the collective Arab consciousness over the past fifty years has been akin, though not identical, to the role that the state of Israel has come to play in the contemporary Jewish identity: One can dislike Israeli leaders and blame them for some of the trouble in which Israel finds itself, and may even dislike Israeli culture, but when Israel is threatened and its survival seems at stake, most Jews cannot help but feel empathy.

The contemporary political consciousness of the region has been largely defined in relation to Israel and Palestine. The creation of Israel in 1948 went against the aspirations of the region as it was recovering from the colonial era. The scar that the 1948 war left on the collective psyche was superseded only by the human tragedy of the Palestinians, most of whom became homeless refugees. The Palestinians were a continuing open wound, a reminder of the magnitude of what had transpired: A small state that most believed was temporary had defeated the collective Arab armies that rejected it. Less than a decade later, Israel joined the Arab world's colonial adversaries, Britain and France, in an attack on Egypt intended to bring down its popular Arab nationalist leader, Gamal Abdel Nasser. A decade later, as Nasser projected hope and promised to recover Arab glory and honor and adopted the issue of Palestine as the central issue for his movement, the dream crashed with a devastating defeat by Israel in the 1967 war. That war was as consequential psychologically to a generation of Arabs as it was objectively tragic to many, especially Palestinians, more of whom became refugees again. Besides the thousands of casualties that Egypt, Syria, and Jordan suffered, and the subsequent devastation of their economies, each lost significant chunks of territory to Israel, and hundreds of thousands of Palestinians in the West Bank and Gaza came under occupation. Thirty-five years later, they remain without independence, an open scar that is a reminder of a painful period of Arab history.

Though Egypt and Syria performed better in another war they waged against Israel in 1973, the outcome of that war served mostly Egyptian, Israeli, and, to a lesser extent, Syrian interests—but not those of the Palestinians. For them, the primary post–1973 war achievement was the acknowledgment by Arab states that Palestinians had the right to represent themselves. A summit conference in Rabat, Morocco, in 1974 recognized the PLO for the first time as the "sole legitimate representative" of the Palestinian people. For years Nasser had chosen to speak for the Palestinians, seeing them as part of the Arab nation of which he saw himself as the leader, and King Hussein of Jordan, much of whose population was Palestinian, had also claimed the right to speak on their behalf. This move of the 1974 summit in essence recognized a separate Palestinian national movement in an Arab region made up of self-serving states.

The most important impact of the 1973 war was that it empowered Egypt to make its own peace with Israel in 1978 without directly preconditioning this peace on a comprehensive settlement in the region or on Israeli withdrawal from other Arab territories occupied in 1967. Regardless of Egypt's objectives, or what errors in decision were made across the region, the outcome was that Egypt's significant weight was no longer thrown into the balance on behalf of other Arab peoples, especially Syrians and Palestinians, in their confrontations with Israel. Without Egypt's military power, no combination of Israel's neighbors had any significant capability to pressure or deter Israel. Even before the full implementation of the Egyptian-Israeli agreement, Israel invaded Lebanon in order to expel the PLO and to help establish a friendly government next door. As Israel besieged the Lebanese capital, Beirut, the inability of Arab states to respond was an immediate reminder of reduced Arab leverage in the shadow of Egyptian-Israeli peace.

As the PLO was forced to move its headquarters away from the borders of Israel to Tunis in North Africa, the mid-1980s were characterized by a new pressing threat to Arab states, especially the oil producers in the Gulf. The Iran-Iraq war, which had started in 1980, began turning to Iran's advantage, leaving many smaller Arab states, including Kuwait, highly concerned. Some, such as the United Arab Emirates, had territorial disputes with Iran, and all feared that its revolutionary government would meddle in their domestic affairs. The Palestinian issue, and the Arab-Israeli issue broadly, were not in the forefront of Arab priorities. In this environment, the Palestinians, frustrated by the inability of Arab states to help end Israel's occupation, took matters into their own hands, launching their first major *intifada* in 1987.

As soon as the Iraq-Iran war ended in 1988, the focus on the issue of Palestine returned, fueled by news from the *in-*

tifada. Reports of Palestinian civilian casualties; confrontations over the important issue of Jerusalem; the rise of the Shamir government in Israel, which was determined to keep the West Bank as part of Israel; and the fear that massive Jewish immigration to Israel would help Shamir implement his strategy led to increased interest in the Arab world. The Iraqi president sought to exploit this public sentiment to his advantage by holding an Arab summit conference in Baghdad at the end of May 1990, just two months before he invaded Kuwait.

Though the United States and Arab governments were able to separate their immediate interests in the Gulf from the Arab-Israeli question and to limit the impact of the issue on the campaign to dislodge Iraq from Kuwait, it was a factor affecting policy, before, during, and after the war. Prior to the war, it limited the ability of Arab governments to face up to Saddam Hussein. During the crisis, the acceleration of the timetable for war came about in part because bloodshed in Jerusalem in the fall of 1990 nearly undermined the U.S.-led coalition. And after the war, the United States moved quickly to fulfill obligations it had incurred during the campaign to proceed aggressively to resolve the Arab-Israeli issue after the end of the conflict. The first Bush administration initiated the Madrid peace process that promised a negotiated settlement of the broader Arab-Israeli conflict.

The psychological breakthrough occurred in 1993, when Israel and the PLO reached a secret agreement in Oslo, Norway. President Bill Clinton invited the Palestinian and

Israeli leaders to a signing ceremony at the White House on September 13, 1993. The agreement stipulated gradual autonomy for Palestinians in the West Bank and Gaza, the establishment of an elected Palestinian Authority, and negotiations to settle all the difficult issues that remained: Palestinian refugees; Israeli security needs; the status of Jerusalem; Palestinian statehood; borders; Jewish settlements that had been built in the occupied territories; and the division of limited resources, especially water. The negotiators hoped that the incremental approach would help build public confidence and enable all parties to move forward, ultimately reaching a final settlement five years after the beginning of the process.

Although most analysts understood that the agreements had many flaws that could undermine the process, most also understood that this was a significant breakthrough in the history of the conflict. The leap forward was less in the details of the agreement than in what the big picture entailed: the parties' mutual acceptance of each other. This political and psychological advance was symbolized by the dramatic handshake between Yitzhak Rabin and Yasser Arafat on the White House lawn on September 13, 1993. The Palestinians accepted Israel's right to exist, and Israel, in accepting the PLO as the representative of the Palestinians, formally acknowledged that the Palestinians constituted a people with national rights. Throughout the decades of conflict, Israelis had rejected the notion that the Palestinians constituted a separate people with a right to self-determination and Palestinians had constantly rejected the notion of Jewish nationalism, seeing Judaism as constituting only a religious and ethnic identity.

The mutual acceptance was significant because it opened up the possibility of territorial compromise to accommodate the fulfillment of the minimal national aspirations of each side in a state of its own. In contrast, in the early years after 1948, when the primary issue for the Palestinians was not one of nationalism but their right to return to their homes inside Israel, this objective was incompatible with the notion of Israel as a Jewish state because the return of all refugees would have resulted in an Arab majority. And previous Israeli positions that had rejected Palestinian nationalism and insisted on keeping most of the West Bank had left no room for accommodating core Palestinian aspirations. The significance of Oslo, therefore, was that it defined the conflict in a way that lent itself to compromise and resolution.

The process of implementation had its ups and downs, with Palestinians gaining autonomy primarily over their cities and Israelis gaining more security. In the end, many flaws in the agreement doomed its realization. The gradual process that was intended to build confidence allowed opponents on both sides opportunities to derail the agreements. Each side, trapped in its own domestic politics, fell far short of honoring its obligations, and the United States, the key broker of the negotiations, failed to hold the participants accountable. Two problems were fatal: The Israelis above all expected a psychology of security, and the Palestinians expected assurances that Israel would ultimately withdraw and allow them to set up an independent state. Yet though violence diminished in comparison to the period prior to the agreement, it nonetheless continued, and suicide bombings inside Israel played to pervasive public insecurities. Of all the Israeli actions in the territories, one shattered Palestinian confidence the most: the continuing construction of Jewish settlements in the West Bank even as the parties were supposedly negotiating Israeli withdrawal from that territory. These mutually self-defeating actions led hard-liners to construct ready-made arguments. In Israel, they argued that the agreements made Palestinian terrorism more possible. Among the Palestinians, they argued that the agreements were a ploy by Israel intended to buy time to consolidate its control by building additional settlements. These fatal features in the implementation of the Oslo agreements were exacerbated by the failure of both governments to prepare their publics for the necessary compromises and to build a mechanism for people-to-people reconciliation—to change the language of enmity that both sides had employed over decades of conflict into a language of peace and reconciliation.

Despite its ups and downs, the process overcame significant hurdles, including the assassination of Israeli Prime Minister Yitzhak Rabin by an Israeli Jew opposed to his moves toward peace, and the election in 1996 of a new Israeli prime minister, Benjamin Netanyahu, who had opposed the Oslo agreements. Despite his tough stance, Netanyahu reluctantly entered into the "Wye River agreement" with the Palestinians, intended to further the implementation of some terms of the Oslo agreement. But the lack of significant progress, continuing violence, and tension between the

Netanyahu government and the Clinton administration assured that Netanyahu's tenure was short. By 1999, he had been replaced as prime minister by Ehud Barak. Barak's election rejuvenated Israel's prospects of reaching a final settlement with the Palestinians, especially because President Clinton was determined to make such an agreement a crowning jewel of his presidency. After a failed attempt at securing a negotiated settlement between Israel and Syria, the stage was set for the Palestinian-Israeli negotiations at Camp David in July 2000.

Before addressing the consequences of the collapse of these negotiations, it is important to keep in mind how the Oslo process changed the regional psychology despite its weaknesses. First, most in the Arab world assumed that the Oslo agreements were ultimately going to lead to Arab-Israeli peace, even if they were uncertain about their actual terms. This assumption enabled many Arab governments to lay the ground for improving relations with Israel and preparing for such peace. Jordan was able to conclude its own peace agreement with Israel. Morocco, Tunisia, Qatar, and Oman began building relations with Israel. Although the violence never fully stopped, the period saw consistent overall drops in Middle Eastern terrorism every year, culminating in the lowest totals by the time of the Camp David conference. Israel was able to focus on its economy and plug into the global economy in a big way, with its standard of living reaching western European levels. The United States, as the broker of the peace, was able to use that role to obtain regional cooperation on its policies elsewhere in the Middle

East, including Iraq, even as it continued to receive criticism in the Arab world for being biased toward Israel.

In the end, the seeming reduction of interest in the Palestinian issue in parts of the Arab world was largely a function of the assumption that the problem was on its way to a resolution. It was akin to discussions among American Jews about the possible decrease of interest in Israel after peace is achieved. These attitudes reflected not lack of interest but shifting priorities that were dependent on subjective assessments of the prospects for peace between Israel and the Palestinians. In that regard, the collapse of the Oslo process in 2000 brought back the urgency of the Palestinian-Israeli issue for both Arabs and Jews worldwide.

The Camp David II Negotiations

It is not my aim to assess what went wrong in Camp David or why the negotiations failed but to put the failure in context and assess its consequences for the Middle East and for U.S. foreign policy.

Several points could help put the outcome of the negotiations in perspective:

1. Each side had a different vision of the negotiations. Since the Israelis were in control of the West Bank and Gaza, they saw every piece of land from which they offered to withdraw as an Israeli concession, as something they were "giving" to the Palestinians. Thus, Is-

rael saw the offer to "give" 90 percent of those lands to the Palestinians as a significant Israeli concession. However, Palestinians believed that in accepting Israel as a state, they had already conceded 78 percent of historic Palestine and were limiting themselves to claiming only the West Best Bank and Gaza, which Israel had occupied in 1967 and to which they felt fully entitled. They saw any portions of these territories that Israel kept, no matter how small, as a Palestinian concession. These different views clearly affected the interpretation of who was compromising more.

2. There was insufficient preparation for the Camp David meeting because the parties had barely discussed such important issues as the fate of Jerusalem and the return of Palestinian refugees.

3. Whereas Barak and Clinton went to Camp David genuinely believing that a full agreement was possible, Arafat didn't feel that the parties were ready. He attended the meeting to see whether progress could be made but did not expect a final deal. For this reason, he first rejected the idea of holding the negotiations but later accepted after President Clinton assured him that no matter what happened, he would not blame the Palestinians in case of failure.

4. Arafat and Barak, who never developed a good working relationship, negotiated mostly through Clinton.

5. There were no written formal proposals put forth during the negotiations, and Israel didn't put forth direct proposals to the Palestinians. The United States conveyed suggestions on behalf of Israel to the Palestinians.

6. Each side presented important new ideas that broke old taboos. Israel began seriously considering compromises on the issue of Jerusalem and was prepared to agree to withdraw from over 90 percent of the occupied territories. The Palestinians agreed to Israeli security arrangements; to the principle that some Jewish settlements in the West Bank would be incorporated into a sovereign Israel; and to Israeli control over parts of East Jerusalem, including the Western Wall, the Jewish Quarters, and Jewish neighborhoods that were built in areas occupied in 1967.

7. Barak wanted to exclude other Arab states from the negotiations, believing there was a better chance for a deal without them, and he persuaded the Clinton administration to go along with that plan.

8. Both Barak and Arafat invoked personal threats to themselves as levers in the negotiations, with Barak reminding Clinton of Rabin's tragic fate and Arafat making it clear that he did not intend to die like Anwar Sadat.

The issue of Jerusalem was the biggest bone of contention, and it partly accounted for the collapse of the talks. Feeling strongly that the focus on Jerusalem was likely to derail the negotiations, I wrote the following analysis in the *Los Angeles Times* on July 14, 2000, at the outset of the negotiations:

Under pressure to reach a comprehensive agreement that would end the Israeli-Palestinian conflict once and for all, both Israel and the Palestinians are insisting at Camp David II that the issue of sovereignty over Jerusalem be settled now. It's a bad idea.

Israel believes that its willingness to make territorial concessions is best employed now to extract maximal Palestinian concessions on Jerusalem. The Palestinians believe that their willingness to end the conflict with Israel at Camp David is their best leverage to regain control over East Jerusalem. But a decision on Jerusalem sovereignty made now is bound to mobilize passionate opposition for one side or the other back home—and may be more than either Ehud Barak or Yasser Arafat can handle.

By "Jerusalem," both Israelis and Palestinians refer largely to the Old City within the ancient walls that houses the most significant holy sites for Jews, Muslims and Christians. The symbolism evoked by these sites cannot be overcome by creative ideas of expanding the city's boundaries.

This symbolism is, in some ways, bigger than the Palestinian-Israeli conflict because it ultimately mobilizes Jewish and Muslim groups from outside the areas controlled by Arafat and Barak.

Emotions run high on both sides when the issue of Jerusalem sovereignty is raised. When pollsters asked Palestinians if they agreed to Israeli sovereignty over East Jerusalem in exchange for Palestinian statehood in the rest of the West Bank and Gaza, an overwhelming majority rejected the Palestinian state if it did not include Jerusalem. In Israel, significant majorities have continually rejected the idea that a Palestinian state would be sovereign over the Old City, and Barak has declared this issue to be one of his red lines. If he were to agree to Palestinian sovereignty over the Old City, the measure would be roundly defeated in Israel.

In the Arab and Muslim worlds, no issue with Israel mobilizes more people. Jerusalem is celebrated and invoked in political, religious and social rallies. The rhetoric in the Arab world on this issue has intensified since the success of the Islamic Hezbollah operations forced the Israeli withdrawal from Lebanon. The dual message of militancy and religion has been put forth as an alternative to negotiations. Giving Israel sovereignty over the walled city would rally groups across the region against the deal. Unlike a powerful Egypt, which was able to withstand a decade of isolation in the Arab world for its 1978 Camp David deal with Israel, Arafat is too weak to prevail without substantial Arab nation support.[3]

In the end the negotiations failed. More importantly, their collapse began unraveling the dominant paradigm of the 1990s: an American-brokered Arab-Israeli peace that would be a cornerstone of a new, stable, and prosperous regional order. Although the reasons for this failure will be long debated, there have been at least two dominant but completely different narratives, one Palestinian and one Israeli, about what transpired, and even members of the American negotiating team are not of one mind about the causes of failure.

It is also important to keep in mind that politicians on all sides have an interest in perpetuating exaggerated interpretations that entirely blame the other side. Given the grave consequences of the collapse, no politician wants to accept responsibility for his or her own mistakes. Immediately after the collapse of the negotiations, I expressed my fears in *The Baltimore Sun* on July 27, 2000, this way: "In their need to exploit the hero's welcome at home for holding firm, Israeli Prime Minister Ehud Barak and Palestinian leader Yasser Arafat will inevitably highlight the other side's shortcomings. In this game, there will be no winners," adding that American politicians "must resist the temptation to blame one side or the other. . . . There will be enough of the blame game in the public discourse here and in the Middle East to endanger the prospects of a future deal."[4] In the process of the focus on blaming the other side, the tragedy becomes not only that each side puts forth a different and exaggerated interpretation of events but that, over time, they come to believe their own exaggerations.

Exacerbating the failure of the negotiations was the breakout of intense violence in the fall of 2000. Predictably, the issue that ignited the passions was the holy sites for Muslims and Jews in Jerusalem. The Barak government agreed to allow Ariel Sharon, the leader of the Likud party, to visit Haram al-Sharif/Temple Mount in Jerusalem on September 28, 2000, accompanied by 1,000 Israeli policemen. The subsequent confrontations with Palestinian demonstrators led to the deaths of four Palestinians and the injuring of 200 as well as the wounding of fourteen Israeli policemen. This incident signaled the revival of the al-Aqsa *intifada*.

Although each side blamed the other, an American-led commission chaired by former Senator George Mitchell concluded that "we were provided with no persuasive evidence that the Sharon visit was anything other than an internal political act; neither were we provided with persuasive evidence that the Palestinian Authority planned the uprising."[5]

Despite the violence, Israelis and Palestinians continued negotiating, making further progress in last-ditch efforts in Taba, Egypt, in December and January but failing to reach an agreement. But the psychology in Israel had turned to the right, leading to Barak's defeat and the election of Ariel Sharon, who was less willing to compromise in his political positions and more determined to employ military instruments to suppress the *intifada*.

Regardless of its causes, the violence had a significant impact on the psychology of Israelis, Palestinians, and Arabs broadly. This psychological dimension has not been sufficiently appreciated by either side of the conflict.

Psychologies of Weakness and Insecurity

To most Arabs, especially Palestinians, Israel is all too powerful: It has repeatedly defeated combined Arab armies; it continues to occupy Arab lands after thirty-five years; it acts freely regarding the Palestinians under occupation; it is backed by the sole remaining superpower, the United States; and it fields one of the most powerful armies in the world with the only nuclear weapons in the Middle East. It is able to withstand international pressure, including UN resolutions, without altering its basic policies. For the Palestinians in particular, especially those under occupation, Israel dominates their daily lives, their economic prospects, their mobility, and their future. They are often at the mercy of the seemingly arbitrary decisions of local military officers. The extent of these feelings of helplessness is not sufficiently appreciated by Israelis, who are trapped by their own pain.

Similarly, the Arab sense of Israeli power has prevented most from coming to grips with the extent to which Israelis feel profoundly insecure. Many Arabs believe that the issue of security is a mere instrument of Israeli foreign policy intended to gain international sympathy for aggressive measures. Although some Israeli leaders and politicians do employ this issue to their advantage, there is a real, pervasive sense of insecurity among most Israelis. In the same way that Arabs have a narrative of victimization because of the way their history unfolded during the twentieth century, Israelis, and many Jews more broadly, have a collective consciousness that is inevitably characterized by insecurity. The horror of the Holocaust has much to do with it, but the history of Israel, seen through Israeli eyes, is also a factor. Regardless of its military and political successes, Israel remains a small, demographically vulnerable state. Whereas Arabs can recover from defeats over time, Israel cannot afford a single defeat.

Although Israelis have made peace with Egypt and Jordan, they fear deep down that Arabs have not really accepted them in the region. This psychology is a central factor in rapid shifts to the right in Israel after events that exacerbate the sense of insecurity. Like the psychology in the Arab world that lends itself to exploitation by ambitious politicians, the Israeli psychology of insecurity is fertile ground for ambitious politicians.

Two Different Narratives

The psychological dimension significantly affected the propensity of the public on each side to accept official narratives. If one looks at the negotiations as an important episode in an ongoing process, one would have to say that much was accomplished at Camp David. The parties narrowed the gap on some important issues further than they had ever done in the previous seven years of negotiations. Yet the expectation that these talks were "the final chance" created a widespread sense of failure.

After the failure to reach agreement at Camp David, there were two dramatically different interpretations of what had happened. The Israeli interpretation is important to understanding the pervasive frustration and despair within Israel and why the Israeli peace camp went on the defensive after the negotiations broke down. In the view of most Israelis, their former Prime Minister Ehud Barak offered the Palestinians the best possible deal and made concessions many didn't think were possible, including on Jerusalem, but Arafat simply rejected the deal without even bothering to counteroffer. Instead of continuing negotiations without violence, this account continues, Arafat encouraged the emergence of the *intifada,* a violent uprising, because he simply did not accept an agreement along these lines and because he thought he could get more through violence. At best, his aim was to force Israel to make more concessions that are unacceptable to Israelis; at worst, he was simply unwilling to accept Israel as a Jewish state and insisted on the right of Palestinian refugees to return to their original homes in Israel, which would turn Israel into a state with an Arab majority. In the end, he wanted not only the West Bank and Gaza but all of Israel.

Although some people didn't accept every detail of this narrative, most Israelis believed most of it. Hence most Israelis, including those who wanted a peaceful settlement, saw no credible option for a negotiated settlement and had no answer to those who wanted to pursue a tough military policy toward the Palestinians. This explains why many Israelis have moved to the right and elected as prime minister Ariel Sharon—a man long associated with ruthless military tactics against the Palestinians. An Israeli commission had found him to be unfit to serve as defense minister because of his indirect responsibility for the 1982 massacre of Palestinians at Sabra and Shatilla by allied Lebanese groups. Suicide bombings against Israeli civilians hardened Israeli views even more.

On the Palestinian side, a completely different narrative explains what happened at Camp David. This interpretation, which was prevalent throughout Palestinian society, was that the Israelis came not to negotiate but to make a "take it or leave it" offer, presenting few concessions and not enough territory to make a viable Palestinian state. In this view, Palestinian leaders made many concessions to the Israelis by accepting that two-thirds of the settlers would remain on West Bank territory annexed by Israel, that parts of East Jerusalem would come under Israeli sovereignty, and that the Palestinians would have a demilitarized state. From their point of view, they had been willing to give up much. However, most Palestinians believe that Israel offered too little, including a state so truncated that it would not have been viable, and no sovereignty over Islamic holy sites in Jerusalem, especially the Haram al-Sharif, the third-holiest place in Islam. Israelis essentially wanted to dictate their own solution instead of proceeding to build on what was already achieved at Camp David: "If you don't accept our terms, there will be no more negotiations." In Palestinian eyes, the Israelis believed they had the power to impose their own solution and thought that the Palestinians, being weak, had no choice but to accept either Israel's terms or continuing occupation. It is clear that, regardless of how spontaneous the *intifada* was, many Palestinians increasingly believed that only violence could help reduce Israel's overwhelming power by sending a message that they are not helpless.

The unfortunate consequence was that moderate Israelis and Palestinians went completely on the defensive while the militants on both sides had their say. Even though polls continued to show that most Israelis and Palestinians favored a compromise peace settlement, most didn't believe such a solution was likely. A horrible cycle of violence began, with civilians as most of the victims on both sides. Two years after the collapse of the negotiations, it was apparent that both sides were in far worse shape than when they had begun and that neither had a unilateral solution.

On the Israeli side, the economy went from boom to bust, exacerbated by the global economic downturn. Military expenditures increased, tourism dramatically dropped, and unemployment rose. The government announced its intent of ruthless measures in the West Bank and Gaza to increase Israeli security, but statistics released by the Israeli police in August 2002 were sobering: In the first six months of 2002, 238 Israelis died in Palestinian attacks, compared with sixty-eight in the corresponding period a year earlier. Those statistics do not include soldiers. In one telling statistic, the police reported that in all of 1999, the last full year before the collapse of the negotiations, twelve bombs were detonated or discovered in Israel. From January 1 though July 18, 2002, the number of bombs was 465. Israelis suffered more than 550 killed and thousands injured in the first two years of the *intifada*. The psychology of insecurity and fear intensified as a result of horrific suicide bombings that took so many civilians' lives.

On the Palestinian side, life became almost unbearable as the economy came to a standstill and poverty became acute. Many Palestinians found themselves under twenty-four-hour curfews that were sustained for long periods. The searches and check-points that limited their travel, sometimes even within a city, made the most ordinary tasks painful and humiliating experiences. And then there were the casualties: In a population of about three million, the number of dead during the two-year period after the collapse of negotiations was more than 1,500, with many thousands wounded and thousands more imprisoned. Above all, there was hopelessness.

Do They Ever Learn?

Given the escalating costs that each side continues to pay, and given that both populations continue to hope that a peaceful solution could be found, will they learn that violence doesn't pay? Will they suddenly change course? Unfortunately, evidence shows that they are unlikely to break out of the cycle on their own.

I have published a study with three colleagues (Joshua Goldstein, Jon Pevehouse, and Deborah Gerner)[6] looking at conflict and cooperation in the Middle East over a twenty-year period (1979–1999). We examined daily data to see how each party reacted to the other party's actions on a daily basis. We found two things: first, that reciprocity becomes the norm as people increasingly behave in a tit-for-tat fashion.

Over time such behavior intensifies and becomes normalized. Second, despite the fact that they were worse off by behaving in a revengeful fashion, cooperation didn't necessarily result from learning that violence didn't pay. Why?

A first answer is domestic politics. When there is an attack on one side, public opinion demands action. People don't accept the fact that they are helpless. They don't accept the fact that they have to sit back. Even if retaliation doesn't pay, domestic political conditions always create pressure toward taking some action, including action that doesn't work—even when the public may realize that it won't work. Revenge is often an end in itself.

Second, there is an insidious belief on each side that not acting is worse than acting; that if one doesn't respond, the other side will interpret the lack of action as weakness and that the nonacting side will therefore be the target of more violence. So even though they know that acting doesn't solve the problem, people often feel that they are better off by acting than by not acting. This is the type of explanation that one hears from parties in conflict in general and is certainly a common attitude expressed by both Israelis and Palestinians.

Third, each side tends to "learn" from the wrong examples in history to rationalize its predisposition to respond in kind. For example, Palestinians say, "Violence worked in Lebanon—the Hezbollah guerrillas were able to force Israel out. Therefore, we can do the same." The obvious differences between the two situations do not prevent people from seeing such parallels. Similarly, many Israelis try to draw parallels between their actions in the Palestinian areas and the seemingly successful U.S. military campaign in Afghanistan, as if the situations are comparable. These rationalizations are driven by the first two tendencies that I suggested above.

These barriers to breaking out of the cycle of violence exist even under ideal circumstances, when the leaders indeed prefer to cooperate. However, the circumstances have been far less than ideal: There is much evidence to suggest that even without these barriers, Ariel Sharon is willing to offer much less than Yasser Arafat previously rejected.

The Dangers Ahead

Rather than learning to cooperate from the failure of violent methods, cooperation will become more difficult as time passes. There are two significant factors that will work against the natural evolution of a solution.

First, there is increasing disbelief in the possibility of coexistence, fueled by ruthless violence and exacerbated by the immediacy conveyed by the new media. Two events shattered much of the psychology of hope on both sides. For the Palestinians, the pictures of a twelve-year-old boy, Muhammad al-Durra, shot to death in the arms of his helpless father on September 30, 2000, conveyed by television stations almost live, was not only a heartbreaking tragedy but a metaphor for their sense of helplessness in the face of Israeli military occupation. For Israelis, the beating to death of two Israelis who strayed into Palestinian areas on October 12, 2000, also captured on camera, evoked deep fears for Israel's security and raised questions about the possibility of coexistence.

The bloodshed in the spring of 2002 has had a broader impact on regional psychology. On the Israeli side, the escalation of suicide bombing, including a horrific bombing in Natanya on Passover that left scores of dead and wounded, created scars that challenge the very notion of coexistence. Among the Palestinians, the ruthlessness of Israeli actions in the West Bank and Gaza, including severe violations of human rights, have increased the urge for revenge. In the Arab world, the live televised images of helpless Palestinians facing Israeli tanks while the world watched has left a mark on the collective consciousness of a new generation that rivals the scars of the 1948 war.

Second, the discussions and debates about the conflict increasingly employ ethnoreligious language instead of the nationalist language that gave rise to possible compromise. Increasingly, Arabs, and Palestinians specifically, speak of "Jews" instead of Israelis, and many Israelis speak of "Arabs" and "Muslims." It is a dangerous and self-defeating phenomenon for both sides. If a solution to the conflict is possible in this generation, hope remains only in the nationalist framing of the conflict: two states for two peoples, one reflecting Jewish nationalism, one Palestinian nationalism. If the conflict is ultimately defined in ethnic or religious terms, it is hard to imagine a solution, at least in this generation. Instead a solution will only become more difficult as the cycle of violence and occupation continues.

Breaking the Cycle

Violence begets violence, and hopelessness, the absence of a genuine alternative to violence, reinforces the cycle. However, despite the difficult circumstances in which Palestinians and Israelis, indeed Arabs and Israelis, find themselves, breakthroughs can happen. Such breakthroughs, the sudden creation of hope, of an alternative course, do occur in history through acts of leadership, either local or international.

Leaders have the capacity to transform the psychology of conflict, to create possibilities through bold acts. But such acts come at a cost: Success is uncertain. Courage is often irrational in the short term, and it is sometimes very costly to the leaders themselves. The two major breakthroughs in the history of the Arab-Israeli conflict—the Egyptian-Israeli treaty and the Oslo agreements—left two courageous leaders, Anwar Sadat and Yitzhak Rabin, dead. However, their actions did transform the possibilities of peaceful reconciliation and broke seemingly impossible taboos. Such acts are possible, but they are historically rare.

Leadership can also come from the outside. Because the Arab-Israeli conflict is consequential not only to Middle Eastern states but also to others, including Europeans, many parties have a stake in what happens. Although most Arab states have not taken direct steps to address the conflict, the escalations in 2002, and these governments' concern about the reaction of their publics on the one hand and about maintaining good relations with the United States on the other has led to new initiatives. In particular, Saudi Arabia put forth a proposal for a comprehensive settlement of the Arab-Israeli conflict, based on full Israeli withdrawal from Arab territories occupied in 1967 in exchange for full peace and normal relations between Israel and all Arab states. Importantly, this proposal was backed by an Arab summit meeting in Beirut, Lebanon, in March 2002. These efforts were also supported by continuing diplomacy by the European Union, which has invested financially in peace, especially in the troubled Palestinian economy.

In the end, no party can achieve results without persuading Israel as well as the Palestinians. And no party has been better placed to influence both sides than the United States—in large part because of its significant economic, military, and political support for Israel and some Arab states; because of its military presence in the region; and because of its global clout as the sole remaining superpower. For these reasons, most in the region see the key to peace as residing ultimately in the White House.

Why America Is the Target of Anger

The view that America holds "99 percent" of the cards has always been exaggerated. Even when the president of the United States places top priority on the goal of achieving peace in the Middle East, as Bill Clinton did during his last year in office, success is by no means assured. But America has a central role to play, and its actions are consequential not only for the Middle East but also for U.S. interests in general. No one other than the parties themselves can affect the outcome more than America.

From the point of view of many in the Middle East, Israel derives its power from U.S. support. Its decisive military edge is in large part owing to America's backing, and although its economy has become less dependent on the United States over time, Israel continues to receive substantial direct and indirect American aid. More importantly, the power of America in international organizations shields Israel from UN Security Council resolutions. Ever since the inception of the United Nations, most of the cases in which the United States has employed or threatened its veto power in the UN Security Council have involved the Arab-Israeli issue. Often the United States has found itself on one side of this issue while all other members of the council were on the other side.

A telling example took place in the spring of 2002, following the Israeli operations in Palestinian cities after a spate of horrific suicide bombings inside Israel. Human rights organizations, including the Israeli B'Tselem, the American–based Human Rights Watch, and the British–based Amnesty International, documented severe violations of human rights, including what some called Israeli war crimes. Pictures were broadcast in much of the world showing great devastation in civilian areas. Arabs accused Israel of "atrocities," especially in the city of Jenin. In this environment, it was hard to know the exact details, but it was clear that there was much death and destruction. With Israeli approval, the Secretary-General of the United Nations announced the establishment of an international commission of inquiry to investigate. As the commission assembled in Europe on its way to the region, Israel decided to deny it entry. The United States went along with Israel's position, resulting in the cancellation of the mission. The resulting resentment toward the United States and the loss of UN credibility were widespread in the region.

One should not underestimate the continued importance of U.S. positions on this issue in shaping perceptions of America not only in the Middle East but also in other parts of the world, especially Europe. While it is not a top-priority matter for most states, the frequency of disagreements over this issue, especially at the United Nations, has become a factor in reinforcing a prevailing negative perception of American unilateralism. It is not a surprise that majorities in places as diverse as Venezuela and France expressed the view in spring 2002 that an American success in bringing about a settlement of this conflict would improve their opinion of the United States.

America's dilemma in its policy toward the Arab-Israeli conflict is that on the one hand, it wants to project an unshakable commitment to Israel's security and well-being, even if it means going against other nations. On the other hand, America's ability to help negotiate a peaceful settlement is undermined by its identification of itself with Israel. This dilemma is exacerbated in times of crisis.

In the end, Israeli and Palestinian leaders must assume much of the responsibility for leading their nations out of a disastrous course. The tragedy of the cycle of violence goes beyond the daily pain of so many innocent, helpless people. It goes even beyond what should be obvious: that neither party will be able to achieve an enduring stable outcome through violence. At stake are existential issues for both sides, and neither will simply wither away. It is also a moral tragedy: Even if one side prevails militarily, the seeming victory will be hollow. What will become of their societies, of their children, as militants and occupiers? America cannot be indifferent, even beyond the moral responsibility that powerful nations have in the face of tragedy and bloodshed. America's interests are at stake: If Israel is weakened or threatened, America will not sit on the sidelines; if Israel gains the upper hand, America will continue to be the object of anger for hundreds of millions of Arabs and Muslims for empowering Israel through military, economic, and political support. This dilemma can be solved only if Arabs and Israelis coexist peacefully. Nor can one ignore continued American strategic interests in the Gulf that are unavoidably affected by the Arab-Israeli conflict. These interests are the subject of the next chapter.

5

The Role of the
Persian Gulf Region

We need to put pressure on Saudi Arabia to change,
but we will not have the leverage to do that as long
as we have a reliance on them for oil. We have to di-
minish that reliance.

—FORMER CIA DIRECTOR JAMES WOOLSEY,
MARCH 5, 2002

In the months following the attacks on U.S. soil, many in our
national debate have inclined toward arguments of wishful
thinking: that the Persian Gulf region is no longer as strategically important as it once was; that Saudi Arabia in particular is less central in the global oil market because of the rise
of new energy powers such as Russia; and that the United
States can significantly reduce its strategic dilemma in the

131

region simply by importing less oil from the Gulf and more from other sources. These arguments miss the central reasons for the continued importance of the Persian Gulf for world energy supplies and the likelihood that it will become even more important in the future.

The discovery that many of the terrorists responsible for the attacks on the United States, including Usama bin Laden himself, came from Saudi Arabia created unusual tension in one of the longest-standing friendly relationships the United States has had in the Middle East—a relationship born from mutual interests in Saudi Arabia's rich oil fields. This friendship endured through the politics of the Cold War, survived the Arab world's own divisions and frustrations with the United States, and outlasted the oil embargo of the mid-1970s. It solidified throughout the Iraq-Iran war and emerged at its strongest in the American-led coalition to compel Iraq out of Kuwait in 1991. Although the United States and the Saudi kingdom have had their disagreements, especially over the Arab-Israeli conflict, both sides have learned to manage the differences for their mutual benefit.

But in the months that followed the attacks on the United States, two things raised the level of tension. First, there was a closer scrutiny of Saudi Arabia's closed political system as people began asking how it could produce the likes of bin Laden. As analysts looked harder, they discovered deep resentment of the United States among Saudis for which their government received a good share of the blame. Many on the American side of the debate believed that the answer was to pressure the Saudi government to confront this anti-

American sentiment and, more importantly, to reform and liberalize its political system. Second, as U.S. support for Israel grew after 9/11 at the same time that the intensity of the Palestinian-Israeli conflict increased, the Arab-Israeli issue became another source of tension.

These tensions ran up against an inescapable reality: that Saudi Arabia remains a central player in the global supply of energy. Hence it was not without leverage in the relationship with the United States. Many U.S. commentators, especially those such as former Central Intelligence Agency (CIA) Director James Woolsey who prefer a unilateral American approach that depends less on building coalitions, grappled to find ways to reduce this dependence. Some went to extremes in suggesting ways to undermine the Saudis, saying they should be treated as enemies rather than friends. One analyst at the RAND Corporation, an American think tank, even briefed Pentagon officials in the summer of 2002 on why the Saudis should be considered enemies and suggested such options as seizing Saudi Arabia's oil fields and freezing its financial assets in the United States. But most of those who wanted to find ways to marginalize Saudi Arabia recommended less extreme measures. A favorite idea was to wean America off Middle Eastern energy sources by finding substitutes for Saudi oil, especially in Russia, whose production was rising and whose role as an oil producer was seen by some analysts as rivaling Saudi Arabia's.

The Caspian Sea area in central Asia has attracted Western interest. A visit to the city of Baku in Azerbaijan on the Caspian Sea in December 2001 called to my mind the fact

that a century ago, that region held half of the world's oil
supplies. Half a century ago, the battle of Stalingrad, one of
the bloodiest of World War II, was fought in large part over
control of those vast supplies. Today the region has little to
show for it. Still relatively poor and underdeveloped, and en-
vironmentally one of the most devastated areas in the world,
it now sees its salvation in the promise of newly discovered
oil reserves. Once again, Western oil companies and political
strategists are showing interest in the region as it embarks on
a project to build a new pipeline through Georgia and
Turkey into the Mediterranean, pumping a million barrels a
day in the hope of meeting projected increases in oil demand and also reducing the impact of the Organization of
Petroleum Exporting Countries (OPEC) on the oil markets.

The Continuing Importance of Gulf Oil

Most scenarios of replacing Middle Eastern oil with other
sources are built on wishful thinking. First, the oil market is
seamless: No matter where the United States buys its oil, any
reduction in the supply will result in price increases everywhere and will affect the entire global economy. The question is not where one buys oil so much as it is who has the
most capacity to supply oil and affect the market. There is no
escaping the fact that the region that has grabbed the greatest global attention during the past half century in matters of
oil, the Middle East, remains critical for future energy supplies. All the scrambling to develop resources elsewhere

around the world can only delay the day of reckoning. Although the Middle East produces a quarter of world oil supplies, it holds between two-thirds and three-quarters of all known oil reserves. For this reason, the United States and other Western nations will have to continue to define the region as vitally important.

It is certainly the case that since the 1970s, the Gulf states' share of the world oil market has dropped as local production levels have slowed and other states have increased their exports. Although natural gas and other energy sources have reduced the relative weight of oil in the global energy market, oil still accounts for 40 percent of the world's energy consumption and is not projected to drop below this level for the next twenty years.

More importantly, barring significant new discoveries of oil, all major increases in oil production from 2010 to 2020 are likely to come from the Persian Gulf as its superior reserves become a central factor in the supply of oil. At the same time, other regions around the world are likely to increase their need for Middle Eastern oil and to compete with the West for these resources. China, for example, now imports 60 percent of the oil it consumes from the Persian Gulf. Forecasts indicate that in the next two decades that figure could increase to 90 percent. China has already begun to invest in energy exploration in Iran and had made efforts to gain development rights in Iraq prior to the 2003 war.

Ultimately, no state around the world has the current impact on and the potential future importance to the oil market of Saudi Arabia—certainly not Russia, whose oil reserves constitute only 5 percent of the global reserves. If the current rate of Russian oil extraction continues, barring any major new discoveries, Russia can expect to deplete its reserve base by 2040. Saudi Arabia's trump card remains its spare production capacity, which allows it to affect the market significantly by withholding or increasing supply. No other country commands such a capacity, and therefore such power, in the global energy market.

Oil and Military Strategy

That the Middle East is vitally important does not automatically lead to the conclusion that a U.S. military strategy is required there. The military dimension of the American oil strategy has recently been an issue of debate in Washington, focused especially on Saudi Arabia, which alone holds a quarter of the world's known oil reserves. One central question has been whether the United States needs to have a military presence in the region at all. Another has been whether our primary aim in maintaining bases in the area has been to defend Saudi Arabia and other Gulf states with whom we now discover we have serious policy disagreements. Many commentators, frustrated with the tension between the United States and Saudi Arabia, have stepped up calls for weaning the United States from foreign oil broadly and Middle Eastern oil in particular. But the debate entirely misses the logic of American involvement.

First of all, buying oil from regions other than the Middle East will not resolve the problem. As the adage reminds us, "we are all sipping from the same cup." The global oil market is largely driven by supply and demand. Middle Eastern supplies affect not only the price of Middle Eastern oil but also the price of global oil. Although the United States can and should conserve energy and develop alternative energy sources, the gap between what the United States now produces and what it consumes (nearly ten million barrels a day) is simply too wide to be bridged in the foreseeable future. The United States should diversify its sources of energy to mitigate the possible short-term impact of interruptions of supply from one source. However, the most important consequences of limiting oil supplies are the effect on global prices of oil and on world economies—and Middle Eastern oil remains critical for these issues. Moreover, the clustering of oil reserves in the Middle East means that at some inescapable point in the not-too-distant future, a greater share of the oil supply will be coming from that region.

Nonetheless, it is not entirely clear why oil economics should be mixed with oil politics or why a military strategy is necessary. Many countries that depend heavily on Middle Eastern oil—such as Japan and many European nations—have assumed that they can base their policy entirely on the demands of the market without a need for political and military intervention. This attitude may in part be driven by their taking the United States for granted and assuming that Uncle Sam will do the job to the benefit of all consumers. But there is more to it than that. Outside the United States, the view is growing that assuring the flow of oil does not require a military approach. This view is bolstered by historical trends. With the exception of the 1973 Arab oil embargo, which was politically motivated and which led to extraordinary increases in oil prices, long-term evidence suggests that the market, more than any other issue, determines trends in oil prices. Historically, political alliances have not greatly altered patterns of trade between the oil-producing countries and the rest of the world. Oil producers sell oil to the countries that need it and that are willing to pay the price. This pattern was true even during the Cold War years, when political relationships were obviously not central to the oil producers' trading behavior. A case in point was Libya, which until 1969 was a strategic ally of the West and hosted British and American military bases. The overthrow of the monarchy in 1969 and the rise of President Qaddafi shifted Libyan politics in favor of the Soviet Union. Yet its trade patterns before and after the coup were largely the same. For example, the share of trade with Soviet bloc nations stood at 1.9 percent in 1960 and 1965, 1.8 percent in 1970, 1.3 percent in 1975, and 1.0 percent in 1980.[1] Moderate states in the Middle East did not differ radically from pro-Soviet states in their trading: The oil-exporting nation with the greatest share of trade with the Soviet bloc was the shah's Iran, not Libya, Algeria, or Iraq. The bottom line was that these states did what was in their economic interest, regardless of their political orientation.

After the 1991 Gulf War, with momentum on the rise for deploying American forces and establishing what amounted to a new fleet in the Gulf, some observers believed that the increased American presence would give the United States a decided advantage over Europe and Japan in trade with the Gulf states. In some instances, no doubt, Washington was able to use its political leverage to help American businesses win contracts in the region, especially in the military and aerospace arenas. But the trade figures between the region and the rest of the world show that the United States had no visible advantage. In 1989, the year before Iraq invaded Kuwait, European exports to the Middle East stood at $40.2 billion, as against $13.7 billion for the United States. In 1992, the year after the Gulf War, Europe's export total was $57.2 billion, as against $19.9 billion for the United States. And the trend continued. In 2000, Europe shipped $63.7 billion of exports to the Middle East, the United States $23.0 billion.[2]

Maintaining a U.S. military presence in the Persian Gulf costs American taxpayers billions of dollars each year. Because these forces can be used elsewhere in the world, that sum is not entirely spent on defending the region. Still, one wonders why the United States devotes so much of its resources, energies, and war planning to the Persian Gulf. Would it not be more sensible to leave the oil issue to market forces and to leave politics and the military out of it?

As conventionally understood, the American strategy is based on a resolve to assure the flow of oil to the West at reasonable prices—a resolve that extends to mitigating short-term interruptions in oil supply and subsequent spikes in pricing by relying on states, notably Saudi Arabia, that have excess capacity. (This notion alone requires Saudi-U.S. cooperation to assure that the Saudi capacity is used as a moderating force on the oil market.) But for more than half a century, a central drive behind the American military strategy in the oil-rich region—one that has been not fully understood by most analysts—has been not to assure continued oil flow to the United States but to deny control of these vast resources to powerful enemies.

The Genesis of the Oil-Denial Policy

As the Cold War was moving to center stage in American foreign policy in 1948, a new worry emerged in the White House: that the Soviet Union could control oil supplies in the Middle East. It is no coincidence that much of the early preoccupation with the potential Soviet threat after the end of World War II centered on the remaining Soviet presence in Iran. Unknown to the public until the declassification in recent years of National Security Council documents was the extent of the Truman administration's concern about a possible Soviet takeover of the oil fields. Equally surprising was that the Truman administration built its strategy not so much on the idea of defending the oil fields in the face of a possible invasion as on denying the Soviet Union use of the oil fields if it should invade.

The National Security Council (NSC) quickly developed a detailed plan that was signed by President Truman in 1949 as NSC 26/2 and later supplemented by a series of additional NSC directives. The plan, developed in coordination with the British government and American and British oil companies without the knowledge of Middle Eastern governments, called for storing explosives in the Middle East. In case of a Soviet invasion, as a last resort, the oil installations and refineries would be blown up and oil fields plugged to make it impossible for the Soviet Union to use them.

The fear that the Soviets might exploit the region's oil was so great that the administration even considered deploying "radiological" weapons. That option was rejected by the CIA, as revealed in another recently declassified document, NSC 26/3, dated June 29, 1950. The explanation was: "Denial of the wells by radiological means can be accomplished to prevent an enemy from utilizing the oil fields, but it could not prevent him from forcing 'expendable' Arabs to enter contaminated areas to open well heads and deplete the reservoirs. Therefore, aside from other effects on the Arab population, it is not considered that radiological means are practicable as a conservation measure."

In other words, the logic of the rejection was that besides denying oil to the enemy, the policy also sought "conservation" of oil, meaning "a preservation of the resources for our own use after our reoccupation." Ultimately, more conventional plugging methods were recommended.

The plan was implemented, and explosives were moved to the region. Although the State Department apparently expressed reservations that the plan might signal that the United States was not prepared to defend the local governments, the fear of Soviet control overwhelmed such concerns. In 1957, the Eisenhower administration reinforced the plan as fears of regional instability grew following the Suez crisis. Evidence suggests that the plan remained in place at least through the early 1960s.

Denying Oil Power to Hostile Regional Regimes

Even during the Cold War, the "oil denial" policy was expanded beyond the perceived direct threat from the Soviet Union. The Eisenhower administration, which faced upheavals in the Middle East that threatened pro-Western governments in the region, began worrying about the emergence of hostile regimes that would control too much power through oil and thus further undermine Western interests. In 1957, following the Suez crisis and its aftermath, which included the overthrow of a pro-Western government in Iraq, the Eisenhower administration expanded the Truman administration's oil-denial strategy. From that point on, the policy pertained to imminent threats not only from the Soviet Union but also from hostile regional governments.

The logic of denying oil to regional powers became a serious factor in America's policy decisions when Iraq invaded Kuwait in 1990. The thought that a powerful Iraq could dominate the oil-rich region was unacceptable to U.S. strategists. It is thus important to review America's policy toward regional powers in its attempt to protect U.S. interests in the Middle East.

Post-British American Strategy in the Gulf

America's increased interest in the Persian Gulf began in the late 1960s as the British were finalizing their withdrawal from the Gulf. At the time there were two significant military powers in the Gulf: Iraq and Iran. The former was ruled by an Arab nationalist government that had been at odds with American foreign policy and was supplied with weapons by the Soviet Union. The latter was ruled by the pro-Western shah, Reza Pahlavi, whose throne had been saved by the CIA in the 1950s, when he faced domestic upheavals. The United States had little chance of deploying major forces in the region to defend Western interests for two reasons: First, the Soviet Union would have resisted such a deployment. Second, and more importantly, the American public was in no mood for such a decision at a time when the United States was trying to disentangle itself from Vietnam. Thus was born the contemporary American approach to Persian Gulf security: balance of power between the two dominant regional powers, Iran and Iraq. Since then no American policy toward one of these states has been contemplated without reassessing the policy toward the other. For the next decade, the United States helped build up Iranian forces, supplying them with modern weapons, especially after Iran benefited financially from the significant increases of oil prices in the mid-1970s. This strategy required little American military presence beyond the reach of U.S. naval forces.

The picture changed dramatically in 1979 when the American-backed Iranian regime was overthrown by a clergy-led popular revolution. Suddenly the two regional powers, Iran and Iraq, were both unfriendly to America, and the one the United States had helped empower was even more unfriendly than the other. Popular anger at America's support of the repressive shah over three decades made Iran a staunchly anti-American country. The hostility was expressed by the taking of American hostages, resulting in a crisis that galvanized the American public for over a year and that contributed to the defeat of President Jimmy Carter in the 1980 presidential elections.

Iraq was at the very same time projecting increasing anti-American sentiment, especially after the United States brokered a separate peace between Egypt and Israel in 1979 that most Arab states rejected. Iraq was a leader of the so-called rejectionist front that refused to accept the bilateral Camp David agreements, which most Arab leaders felt came at the expense of their interests. Iran and Iraq competed during that period to champion the Palestinian cause. Even though Iran is a non-Arab Shiite Muslim state, its spiritual leader, the Ayatullah Ruhollah Khomeini, highlighted the spiritual importance of Jerusalem, and one of his first acts was to close the Israeli embassy and open one for the Palestine Liberation Organization.

The 1979 Soviet invasion of Afghanistan to save the besieged communist government in Kabul made matters seem even more threatening to American interests. This invasion revived U.S. fears dating back to the beginning of the Cold War that the Soviet Union aspired to a foothold in the Gulf. These perceived threats propelled the Carter administration to declare the Gulf region as being "vitally important" to the United States as a way of preempting any Soviet designs to exploit the changed strategic environment.

Many American analysts often lump Arab and Muslim states together. They assume that these states' motivation in regard to America is the single most important issue driving their foreign policies. But the events that transpired immediately after 1979 were a reminder that Iran and Iraq disliked and feared each other even more than they were angry with America. Iran was led by a government of Shiite Islamic clergy who had always opposed the secular Baathist government in Iraq. The Iraqi government's treatment of the marginalized Shiite majority, with whom Iran had religious and cultural ties, was also a point of dispute.

After months of tension over the disputed Shatt-al-Arab waterway that separates the two countries, during which Baghdad accused the Iranian revolutionary government of attempts to sow dissent in Iraq, Saddam Hussein's government launched a war against its neighbor. That war lasted eight years and cost both countries significant losses both in lives and purse. Nonetheless, it was not seen in Washington as especially threatening. Throughout that period, the U.S. outlook was that these two unfriendly states were undermining each other's capabilities to threaten American interests. American policy thus had two primary objectives. First, the war could not spill over to other parts of the Gulf, especially to Saudi Arabia, Kuwait, and the other small Gulf nations, in a way that would undermine the supply of oil. Second, the United States did not want to see a clear winner in the war lest a dominant power emerge with whom the United States would have to contend. Above all, the United States did not want to see an Iranian victory, both because it feared the Islamic revolutionary government in Iran a bit more than Saddam Hussein and because America's Arab friends in the Gulf, including Saudi Arabia, supported Iraq.

When Iraq seemed to gain the upper hand in the war, the Reagan administration, despite its strong public opposition to Iran, secretly began negotiations to supply Iran with weapons in exchange for its cooperation in securing the release of American hostages in Lebanon. Arms transfers in fact took place, beginning in 1985 with the shipment to Iran of American antitank missiles, provided through Israel. Later U.S. officials began worrying about the changing tide of the war, especially in 1986, when the Iranians seemed to overcome their early losses and gain an edge that led some analysts to conclude that time was on Iran's side. After Iranian forces took the Iraqi Faw Peninsula, near Kuwait, in 1986, U.S. analysts feared that the war might expand to affect Kuwait and shipments of oil. In 1987, the United States signaled its commitment to securing the flow of oil by reflagging Kuwaiti ships (with American flags) and providing U.S. Navy protection for them, thus sending a strong message that an attack on these ships would be an attack on America. In addition, the United States began helping Iraq militarily, all in the name of keeping a balance of power in the Gulf. The war ended in 1988 with an Iraqi advantage, though it was a stretch to call it a major military victory for Iraq. To be sure, the war ended when Iran accepted UN plans for a cease-fire, even though it had taken the position that it would never do so while the Baathist government remained in Baghdad. The decision was thus difficult for Iran's Khomeini, a bitter enemy of Saddam Hussein, who compared accepting the cease-fire while Saddam was still in power to "drinking a cup of poison." But the Iranian decision was made because by 1988 Iraq had the upper military hand, and there was little prospect of Iran turning the tide again.

At the same time, Iraq was devastated by that war. However, even without any territorial gains, the appearance of military victory and improvements in Iraq's missile capabilities enabled Saddam Hussein and his government to exploit the end of the war as a major military and political victory.

The Consequences of the 1991 Gulf War

In the months between the end of the Iraq-Iran war and Iraq's invasion of Kuwait in August 1990, the Cold War between the Soviet Union and the United States was coming to an end, and the fear of a Soviet threat in the Gulf had all but disappeared.

Iraq's invasion of Kuwait completely changed the strategic outlook for the United States. Although the early American rhetoric focused on the rules of international relations in the post–Cold War era, the primary fear was the end of the balance of power in the Gulf. If Iraq were allowed to get away with its occupation of Kuwait, it would double its oil capacity overnight and become the most significant power in the Middle East, next to Israel. Even if it did not employ that power to invade Saudi Arabia or the smaller Gulf states, and thus dominate the region, it would be in a position to intimidate them and dictate their policies. The thought that Iraq—whose foreign policy generally was at odds with America's, especially on the issue of Israel—would become such a significant power was probably the primary force behind the American reaction. The central U.S. argument on behalf of maintaining a strict international economic sanctions policy against Iraq after the war was that if Iraq were allowed to have more income at its disposal, it would employ that income to bypass military sanctions and build up its forces.

The 1991 Gulf War resulted in a significant new development: a large number of American forces in the region and the establishment of new military bases in several Arab states, including Kuwait, Bahrain, Saudi Arabia, the United Arab Emirates, and Qatar. But the United States continued to view Iran and Iraq through the prism of the balance of power between the two countries. The defeat of Iraq in 1991, its reduced power, and the imposition of stringent sanctions that have further eroded its power throughout the 1990s raised concerns about Iran. U.S. foreign policy in the past several decades has never envisioned one of the two except in relation to the other. Any new Iraq policy also necessitated change in policy toward Iran. The strategic goal of American policy after 1991 was to preserve the territorial integrity of Iraq lest it be too weakened in relation to Iran while at the same time finding ways to limit Iran's power while Iraq is weak. This logic came to be known as "dual containment," the policy pursued by the Clinton administration. The argument for that policy was that neither Iran nor Iraq were friendly states, and since Iraq was to be kept under tight sanctions, Iranian power must also be contained. Thus, the United States announced measures prohibiting American companies from dealing with Iran and worked hard to persuade its European allies to do the same. President George W. Bush's policy of including Iran (with Iraq and North Korea) as a member of "the axis of evil," despite Tehran's cooperation with the United States in the first phase of the war on terrorism, was an inevitable outcome of considering a war with Iraq. The United States has grievances with Iran, but no new factor warranted the sudden hardening of policy except the new outlook that the administration developed toward the Gulf. Plans for war with Iraq raised fears of increased Iranian power among the smaller Arab Gulf states, whose support the United States desired in its Iraq policy. The short-term consequence of the war was the reduction of Iraq's military power, thus raising the American concern that Iran might benefit strategically.

The extent to which Iraq and Iran posed significant threats will remain a matter of debate. Did they pose direct threats to the United States that could not be contained? Or was the U.S. concerned more for America's friends in the region, especially Israel? The central argument made by the Bush administration in defining the "axis of evil" was the notion that states like Iran and Iraq were dangerous because they sought to acquire weapons of mass destruction and because they could provide such weapons to terrorists—thus threatening America and its friends. These arguments assumed that deterrence, which worked against the Stalinist USSR and Maoist China, would not work against these states; that their regimes hated America more than they wished to survive; and that they were connected to the terrorists that attacked the United States. The latter point has been very difficult to support, especially because none of the terrorists involved in the 9/11 attacks came from Iran or Iraq and because al-Qaeda and its backers, the Taliban regime in Afghanistan, were friends of neither state. A better case could be made that these states posed a threat to Israel.

It was hard to imagine circumstances under which Saddam's government in Iraq and the Islamic government in Iran would have been seen by Americans as anything but aggressive, especially since President Bush had declared them part of the "axis of evil," which became a central feature in the war on terrorism, and introduced a policy of "preemption." This outlook made it likely that the United States would continue to prevent these two states from dominating the bulk of the world's known oil reserves.

The Consequences of the Iraq War

Regardless of the short term results of the war in Iraq, the long-term questions are much bigger: How will the United States protect its oil interests in the region? How will it minimize the chance of terrorist attacks on its own soil? How will it maintain its support for Israel? Most in the American debate had generally accepted the desirability of bringing about regime change in Iraq, and possibly Iran, and that the Saudis must be pressured to democratize as a way of minimizing militant opposition. Indeed, as in the case of Mr. Woolsey, some viewed war with Iraq not only as a way of preempting that country's nuclear capabilities but also as a way of gaining leverage against Saudi Arabia by reducing the need for U.S. military facilities there and increasing the role of an American-friendly Iraq in the oil market.

The influential *Financial Times* of London, on August 11, 2002, summarized the assumptions of this influential school of thought that sought to order the Middle East through the exercise of overwhelming force. Noting that "Washington's European and Arab friends" suspected that the Bush administration's "campaign to bring down Saddam Hussein is in reality part of a strategy to reorder the Middle East in America's interest and for Israel's benefit, using control of Baghdad as the lever," it concluded, "Administration hawks have long argued that this should be the strategy. Achieving it, after all, would not only deal with the potential threat of Mr. Hussein's weapons of mass destruction. Control of Iraq would lessen U.S. dependence on Saudi oil, continue the encirclement of Iran, put enormous pressure on Syria, and even marginalize Egypt, another U.S. ally."

It is doubtful that there was unanimity among U.S. policymakers about the aims of U.S. policy in a post–Saddam Hussein Iraq. However, it is clear that the dominant vision was the overt employment of American power to change the strategic picture. The argument was that by winning a war with Iraq, the United States would turn that important country into an American ally, which would automatically change the calculations of all its neighbors. Iraq is a potentially rich country with an industrious people who are well educated and secularized. It has historically played a key role in regional politics. It holds the second-largest oil reserves in the world. A friendly Iraq bordering three other friendly states, Kuwait, Jordan, and Turkey, would intimidate the other two bordering states, Syria and Iran. The oil potential of Kuwait and Iraq combined with the other smaller oil producers in the Gulf would rival Saudi Arabia's potential. If one adds the enhanced American military presence in the region, the prospect was alluring to many Washington analysts and decision makers.

According to this line of thinking, it was unnecessary to be concerned about international opposition, including in the Middle East, because once the policy was implemented, others would simply have to adapt. There was little doubt that the United States would win any military confrontation with either Iran or Iraq, or, for that matter, any combination of states in the region. Most states, especially weaker ones, did not want to be on the wrong side of the winner. Therefore, the assumption was that many states opposing such a scenario would simply jump on the winning bandwagon, and those who didn't would suffer severe consequences.

To add allure to this vision, many advocating it suggested that such a scenario not only would reduce the threat of weapons of mass destruction but also would help transform the region from authoritarian rule to democracy. America would be able to assure the emergence of a democratic Iraq and increase its leverage against states such as Egypt and Saudi Arabia, thus forcing them to change internally—both because their people would see the success of democracy in Iraq and because the United States would be better able to pressure their governments. Such changes would lead to a more stable Middle East and to a reduction of terrorism, since the prevailing assumption was that repression fostered terrorism.

Concerns About the War's Consequences

There was never doubt that the exercise of overwhelming U.S. force in the Middle East could change power configurations in the region and the calculations of every state. There was also little doubt that if the United States were willing to deploy enough of its resources with the aim of changing governments in Iraq, and even Iran, it would succeed. But there were a number of concerns expressed before the war about the cost of such missions and about the size of the coalition the United States could build. Many states, including those that opposed and feared such a scenario, were likely to reconcile themselves to it if they had no choice. Power remains central in ordering international politics and reshuffling the priorities of states. But one issue that power cannot settle is the ultimate consequences of its being exercised, the long-term impact on the calculations of local and global actors. The United States has the power to reshuffle the deck in the Middle East but not to determine how the cards will fall.

The argument that the exercise of military and political power would transform the region from authoritarianism to democracy went counter to the logic of realpolitik both for America and for the regional actors—and it also went against historical evidence. The primary aim was to assure a stable Iraq that is friendly to America and to protect the lives of Americans stationed in the area. This in itself was no small task, given the divisions within Iraq and the influence and interest of some of its neighbors, such as Iran, Turkey, and Syria. Iraq was a devastated country after two full decades of war and economic sanctions and would require considerable reconstruction before it could reap the benefits of its potential. This task, together with the central American priority of preventing terror attacks against the United States, was bound to outweigh all else, including the issue of democracy. Would we allow the long-repressed Shiite majority in Iraq, which has strong religious ties with Iran's Shiite majority, to exercise its democratic power if it turned out that it would be sympathetic to Iran? In our attempt to secure backing from the Jordanian monarchy next door, should we not look the other way if the only way the king could lend his support to America was by repressing his public, which strongly opposed the war and the American presence? Consider our recent relationship with Pakistan, whose support we desperately needed in the war against al-Qaeda and the Taliban regime. The need for such support overwhelmed any U.S. desire for significant democratic change in Pakistan. Historically, realpolitik calculations have raised fears that democratization would lead to the emergence of radical anti-American governments in the region. At the least, such calculations have inclined us to overlook domestic politics in seeking essential alliances. Even though the United States may wish to see democratic change in Saudi Arabia, would it accept a radical Islamist government that could use the power of oil and the pulpit of Mecca, where millions of Muslim pilgrims go every year, to rally other Muslims to its cause? There was nothing to suggest that this historical pattern would not be the pattern in the future regardless of what happened in post-war Iraq.

The public perception of the United States in much of the Arab and Muslim world was of American imperialism. Increased and visible U.S. military force in the oil-rich regions of the Arab and Muslim was bound to intensify public resentment of American foreign policy. Governments had two choices: either avoid America's wrath by repressing the public or avoid their public's wrath by annoying America. Either choice was not likely to have a happy outcome for regional politics or for American objectives. In those countries caught in the middle, unable to make up their minds, the resulting instability will be a fertile ground for terrorists. The pervasive psychological humiliation among a new generation of young Arabs and Muslims, connected to America, may in the long term be the most worrisome consequence.

In addition to the issues of repression, public opinion, and resentment of America among a new generation of Arabs and Muslims, there will also be uncertainty about the ability to bring about stability in Iraq and the countries surrounding it. There is little doubt that Iraqis have suffered tremendously under the rule of Saddam Hussein, and most probably looked forward to the day when they would be rid of his regime. But as soon as the dust settled after the war, the reality of internal divisions and external interests significantly complicated America's task. At a minimum, large economic and military resources needed to be employed in a sustained fashion over a long period to assure success.

Despite the obvious risks and potentially severe consequences, the arguments for employing overwhelming power to reorder politics in the region was too much to resist. It is always difficult to present an alternative view based simply on fear of consequences because these are always debatable. Those who argued for the use of overwhelming power had much going for them: What they promised resonated with many Americans, and our ability to succeed in the military phase was assured. For them, "we can, therefore we should" was a sufficient argument.

Had the consequences of an invasion turned out to be severe, such as the possible use of weapons of mass destruction by Iraq, then it would have been easy to suggest that the Iraqis deserved attack before they obtained even more lethal weapons. However, if Iraq were to turn out to be as weak as most analysts suspected (and as the war indeed proved it to be), that weakness would refute the arguments of those who warned of the difficulty of overthrowing its current government. In either case, the deck seemed stacked in favor of those who advocated the use of overwhelming force against Iraq. As for long-term consequences, few Americans would remember in the future where it all started. And if the consequences were especially painful, the pain could prevent us from accepting even partial responsibility lest such an acknowledgment seem to justify the ugly acts that generated such pain. At least that was the hope of the war's proponents.

But it was highly irresponsible to ignore the consequences of our actions, both in the short and long terms, and when the outcome was not to our liking to pretend that we had little to do with the consequences. An approach that focuses on power alone must also recognize, by definition, where much responsibility lies. With power comes substantial influence but also much responsibility. We have certainly helped shape the current political order in the Middle East. We possess the power to reorder politics in the region, to ignore the wishes of its people, to compel others to adjust to new realities that we create, but this power demands that we hold our own leaders accountable, even when there is much pain. Above all, we must contemplate the effects of our policies.

Iraq's conventional resources were never a match for American power, though there had been serious and legitimate worries before the war. Had the Iraqi regime possessed serious weapons of mass destruction, as the U.S. government argued, it would probably have used them when its own destruction was imminent. Such weapons would have significantly increased casualties for America and its allies. In war, there are always surprises. Iraq burned the Kuwaiti oil fields as it retreated in the 1991 war. It could have had an effective plan to burn its oil fields to render them unusable so as to prevent the United States from reaping strategic benefits. Fortunately, Iraq appeared to have no usable weapons of mass destruction, and the damage to the oil fields was minor, but the risks were great if one believed government estimates.

As for the aftermath of the war, although most Iraqis were probably happy to be rid of their repressive government and welcomed change, many did not. Moreover, hatred of the Iraqi regime did not by any means translate into a love of the United States or its policies, so the challenge of maintaining a unified, stable, and friendly Iraq should not be underestimated. Was it wise to ignore the fact that our actions would intensify hostility, anger, and a sense of deep humiliation for a new generation of Arabs and Muslims? Was it in our interest to be seen as the new imperialist in a region whose contemporary history is defined by hatred of imperialism?

Saudi Arabia and the Need for Political and Economic Reform

It is useful to begin addressing the changing American view of Saudi Arabia with the immediate issue for American foreign policy: the war on terrorism. Much of the official frustration with Saudi Arabia since the 9/11 attacks has been predicated on two assumptions: first, that the Saudis have helped create al-Qaeda by encouraging, or at least not discouraging, anti-American rhetoric in the kingdom; and second, that the closed Saudi monarchic system, which allows little legitimate political dissent and accords religious fundamentalist groups considerable cultural power, radicalizes opposition groups and increases the chance of terrorism. U.S. support for the royal family is seen as a central reason why these groups target America.

Though the Saudis have unwittingly helped create al-Qaeda, and must therefore address the internal causes for its rise, we must put this phenomenon in perspective. Al-Qaeda is a threat not only to the United States but also to the Saudi government; its aim is to overthrow the Saudi regime as much as to hurt America. The Saudis had a role in creating this Frankenstein's monster, but the United States had a significant hand in it too. In fact, America played a greater role than Saudi Arabia in the political origins of Usama bin Laden and his horrible organization. U.S. efforts to mobilize devout Muslim political activists across the globe in the name of jihad against the "infidel" communists in Afghanistan was a central reason for the early success of these groups, which ultimately helped form al-Qaeda. The role that countries such as Saudi Arabia and Egypt played to help recruit such people was in large part in response to U.S. wishes.

Regardless of the roots of al-Qaeda, there is a strong case for the need to reform an authoritarian regional system that has radicalized domestic opposition. An argument can be made that extreme repression increases the likelihood of violent opposition, including terrorism. But the record is by no means clear on this point. In the Middle East in particular, results have actually been mixed regarding the extent to which repression increases or decreases violent opposition. Syria, which ruthlessly confronted Islamic opposition groups in the 1980s, seems to have succeeded in quelling militancy. In Jordan, modest political liberalization that allowed Islamic parties to participate in politics has also reduced the incidence of violent dissent.

Nonetheless, democracy in Saudi Arabia and the rest of the region would be good in itself and would have at least one important stabilizing effect on the political system in the region: bolstering the identity of states at the expense of pan-Arab and pan-Islamic identities. When the legitimacy of the government is based on elections by its own people, it needs to appeal less to regional causes as proof of its legitimacy.

But if the end result of democracy is desirable, the means of getting there are the subject of continued debate among experts. One conclusion that can be drawn from historical cases is that even if democracy leads to more stability, *transitions* to democracy are often extremely unstable and, in the end, unpredictable. Rapid radical transitions from authoritarianism to democracy in places such as Saudi Arabia are unlikely, but were they to occur, the resulting instability or unpredictable outcomes, such as the possibility of a militant Islamist regime being democratically elected, may seem even more threatening to American interests than the status quo.

A constructive approach is to seek incremental change. Such change can be achieved only through a mutually beneficial, collaborative effort with others, including willing governments in the region. For many reasons, rulers in the region, whose propensity to keep power remains undiminished, at the same time feel the need to change, especially in the economic arena. The role of the United States should be to increase their incentive to bring about such change.

It is important to understand the roots of authoritarianism in the region generally as we seek to help the forces of change. First, the historical path began with the installment of authoritarian regimes by the colonial powers. Such paths are difficult to change because those who hold power are rarely willing to give it up. In some important ways, the region has been hostage to this unfortunate situation because rulers see their positions as entitlements. The problem has been exacerbated by the insecurities of most governments in their early years as they created new identities around new states at a time when the challenges from transnational movements (pan-Arabism especially) were strong. As they built loyalties, it became harder to separate "state" and "ruler." Second, the economic system has helped reinforce authoritarianism, in the Gulf in particular. Oil wealth has assured that governments do not depend on their publics through taxation for income because most of the states' income comes directly from national resources. That substantial income has been employed to influence the public, which has come to expect governments to provide for their needs. This economic structure worked when there was an overabundance of oil, but it has been less effective in the past decade because of rapidly increasing populations and declining per capita income. The resulting pressures present governments in the region with important internal reasons to seek political change to spread the responsibility. If they don't, they will have to worry about militant opposition even more than America does.

Although there are historical and domestic reasons for the continuation of authoritarianism in the region, foreign policy has also been a considerable factor in recent years. In the 1950s and 1960s, states such as Nasserist Egypt used confrontation with Israel as an excuse for secrecy, repression of dissent, and economic failures. In recent years, the Arab-Israeli conflict has worked against liberalization in countries friendly to the United States, such as Saudi Arabia. The core issues of foreign policy for the Saudi public, especially the Arab-Israeli conflict, are the biggest source of resentment of the United States and present many of the governments in the region with tough choices between pleasing America or pleasing their people. Most often, they have pleased neither perfectly but have pleased their publics the least. Consider, for example, the reaction of the Arab public to American foreign policy during the period of intense Palestinian-Israeli violence in the spring of 2002. The response of the Arab public, which perceived its own governments as either impotent or collaborators with the United States, inclined governments to deploy significant security resources to prevent serious internal threats. As in the past, the governments have succeeded, but only at the cost of additional repression in the short term and lasting repression in the long term. The establishment of effective, large state security bureaucracies itself becomes a factor in the domestic political system that hinders change. If one considers the frequency of such episodes, one can understand the extent to which foreign policy issues, especially the Arab-Israeli conflict, have been an important factor in perpetuating repression.

In the end, the goal of achieving more democracy in the region is complex and challenging. Though the United States can play a role in a process of political reform in the region, no power can bring it about alone. Governments in the region will not happily accommodate plans to undermine their power. A threatening, confrontational strategy creates the dual risk of alienating or destabilizing more states in the region. Neither outcome is a happy one for the war on terrorism: Alienated states are less likely to provide the cooperation the United States needs to battle terrorism, and unstable states may provide fertile grounds for terrorists.

The most promising approach to bringing about gradual political reform in the region, without significantly increasing instability in the process, is to begin by focusing on reform in the economic and educational systems. All states in the region, including the oil-rich ones, are facing serious economic challenges that contribute to the political threats against them. They need to liberalize their centralized economies, attract foreign investment, and create an environment hospitable to international business. The United States can help in these areas, but governments also have their own incentives to pursue these goals, such as the hope of improving their troubled economies. Internal demand for political reform will increase as economic reform takes hold, and the United States could continue to assist the voices of reform in the region.

The states of the Gulf Cooperation Council (GCC)—Saudi Arabia, Kuwait, Bahrain, the United Arab Emirates, Qatar, and Oman—continue to have interests in maintaining close relations with the United States, especially American military support. That interest gives the United States some leverage, but only up to a point because the GCC states know that the U.S. strategy primarily serves America's own interests. The result is clear mutual incentives to cooperate. When threats to oil are clear, as in the case of the Iraqi invasion of Kuwait in 1990, Saudi Arabia and other GCC states will undoubtedly rally behind the United States to defend the oil fields. Even without an imminent threat, GCC states, especially Kuwait, have an interest in the U.S. presence in the region. U.S. forces are spread throughout much of the

Gulf, from prepositioned equipment in Qatar to forces and equipment in Kuwait to naval facilities in Bahrain. Saudi Arabia, which also hosts American troops, has incentives to maintain an American presence in the region because it cannot face Iran or Iraq on its own, even as it seeks to reduce the numbers and the profile of American forces on its soil for fear of public backlash.

Historically, people of the Arabian Peninsula have been fiercely independent—and not just in their relations with the West. In the nineteenth century, they challenged the Ottoman rulers, who controlled much of the Middle East in the name of an Islamic empire dominated by Ottoman Turks. In the early twentieth century, they cooperated with Britain in World War I in order to achieve independence from the Ottomans. They joined the American-led coalition in 1990 because they feared being dominated by Saddam Hussein. Their pursuit of independence was not a function of whether the feared powers or the potential allies were Muslim, Arab, or Western.

Much of the resentment of the United States is based on the Arab-Israeli conflict, which has been a visible sore point in the U.S.-Saudi relationship since the collapse of Arab-Israeli peace negotiations. As recent surveys have indicated, most Saudis, like other Arabs, resent America for its policies, not its values, and they see the Palestinian issue as a central issue of contention.

In the months since September 11, the Saudis have discovered that the popular perception of the illegitimacy of the American presence on their soil is a threat to them as

well as to that presence—and the United States is also dis-
covering the depth of public resentment in the region. This
problem will necessitate mutual cooperation. The Saudis will
continue to need American backing, and the United States
will continue to gain more from Saudi cooperation than from
confrontation.

6

The Prudence of Compassion

When I was an undergrad, I worked in several restau-
rants, including some fancy ones; let's just say that
I'm convinced that it's a good idea to be nice to the
waiting staff. You don't have to make them rich, or
cower before them, or let them live in your neighborhood. . . . Respect gets good results.

—FROM A READER'S COMMENTS ON AN
ARTICLE I WROTE

American interests in the Middle East will continue to be
important in U.S. policy into the next decade and beyond.
The commitment to Israel binds America to the Middle East
in inescapable ways, and the continued importance of oil for
the world economy, coupled with the region's domination of
the world's oil reserves, means that the Middle East will remain strategically important to America. The concern about

the threat of terrorism and the likely continued presence of American military forces in the region add another level of interest. The question for America is how to manage these important interests in the coming years. The stakes are high.

The United States will be constantly lured by an approach that relies primarily on America's obvious advantages as the sole remaining superpower because a deeply pained public is hoping for quick and simple answers. This approach focuses largely on using U.S. military power to address the challenges America faces and on dealing with governments alone, through incentives and threats, without concern for world public opinion. It seeks to pursue American interests in the region with little regard for the vital interests of others and sees the war on terrorism as primarily an American issue—or at least one whose definition is a unilateral American right.

America remains strong and capable. In confronting other states militarily, it surely will prevail, even when it goes it alone. In exercising such power, it will inevitably reshape the priorities of other states and, as in the Middle East, even remake the regional political order.

But the dilemma of the exercise of power is that defeating others is not always the same as winning. There are many reasons to be concerned that such an approach applied to the Middle East will hurt not only America's enemies but also its friends and in the end may undermine the very interests that we are trying to defend. There are four main reasons to be concerned:

1. Underestimating the limitations of power

2. Motivating others to challenge America

3. Mischaracterizing the nature of the challenge faced, and thus the nature of the necessary response

4. Overlooking the values at stake, what we stand for as a nation

Articulating these four concerns is the aim of this final chapter.

1. Limitations of Power

It is gratifying to be the most powerful nation on earth, to deter potential enemies and to punish those who attack us on our own soil. The ability to punish those who were behind the crimes of 9/11 has been not only cathartic but also necessary for preventing other attacks. Both the threat and the exercise of power are important in achieving national goals and securing global stability—and they are both sometimes unavoidable.

At the same time, it should be clear that although power is an important asset for prudent diplomacy, it is not a replacement for diplomacy. We have more power than anyone else, but this power is not unlimited. Others too wield power and have the potential to wield more. In exercising power, we must always calculate not only the likely short-term benefits but also the long-term consequences for our ability to exercise it again. Making more enemies than friends is inefficient and imprudent.

Consider the Iraq war of 2003, carried out with minimal support from others and in the face of opposition from many countries in the region and around the world. The United States succeeded in overthrowing the government in Iraq, even if its action was nearly unilateral. But to assure a favorable outcome in the long term, the United States needed to commit significant economic, military, and political resources for an extended period. The fact that the task required such resources at the same time that America was continuing its global war on terrorism, especially in central Asia, diminished America's ability to undertake additional campaigns elsewhere. It could undermine the coalition the United States needs for the success of its antiterrorism campaign. If the intent of a strategy of this sort was in part to exhibit America's overwhelming power and Washington's willingness to employ it so as to deter potential enemies, the result may in the end be overextension—the Achilles' heel of many empires. America's ability to deter new threats to its interests would be undermined. This is the dilemma of power: It is most effective when it is least used; the more one uses it, the fewer the remaining resources and the less credible the threat of its use.

It is also important to consider the effect of the war with Iraq on many around the world who were increasingly

resentful of American unilateralism: they became more motivated to forge coalitions to reduce the impact of American
power. States aspiring to acquire nuclear weapons—such as
North Korea and Iran—have accelerated their efforts in an
attempt to deter American unilateralism. If American unilateralism is replicated by other regional powers, the consequences for the global order will be even more challenging.

2. Motivating Others to Challenge America

Military strategists have long understood that a central issue
in the outcome of any conflict is motivation, both one's own
and that of the adversary. The extent to which a cause is seen
as more or less "legitimate" internationally affects the degree
of the parties' motivation. Military power is obviously central
in the outcome, but in the long term the importance of motivation balances the importance of military power. As a
stronger party's will to fight or to accept even limited casualties decreases, the will of its weaker opponent increases and
its threshold of pain rises. The contrast between Israel's experience in Lebanon on the one hand and its confrontations
with Palestinians on the other may prove instructive.

Israel withdrew from Lebanon in 1999 after years of occupation. Although the lesson learned by some in the region
was that guerrilla warfare works against Israel because of the
perception that Israel was militarily defeated by the
Lebanese Hezbollah group, the outcome was in large part a
function of each party's motivation. Militarily, Israel pos-

sessed overwhelming power vis-à-vis Hezbollah, the Lebanese state, and its domineering neighbor, Syria. Hezbollah forces numbered in the hundreds and had limited equipment. Israel not only had decisive military advantages but also inflicted considerably more pain on Hezbollah and on Lebanon (and sometimes on Syrian forces) than was inflicted on it. Because of Israeli actions, Lebanon faced the creation of tens of thousands of refugees; hundreds of casualties; and the serious undermining of its economy through such methods as the destruction of power stations that paralyzed its capital, Beirut. In contrast, Israel's economy was minimally damaged by its presence in southern Lebanon, and the number of casualties it sustained was small by the measures of warfare (a few dozen a year). Israel could have afforded to continue its presence, and many within Israel's military establishment did not want to pull out of Lebanon without a peace agreement.

However, in the end, Israel did withdraw without such an agreement. Hezbollah members and others in the region interpreted this result as a military victory that could be replicated in the Palestinian areas. This conclusion was an erroneous and unfortunate interpretation. Israel's withdrawal and Hezbollah's success simply cannot be understood by the power equation alone, or by the usual measures of winning or losing a war. At issue was each side's motivation. More importantly, the degree of motivation was a function of two factors that are not directly related to power: the extent to which the conflict was seen by each side as vitally important to its existence and the extent to which the cause was perceived as legitimate in international eyes.

The fact that Israel occupied Lebanese lands and operated from them was seen by most Lebanese, including those who opposed Hezbollah, as a threat to their sovereignty that superseded any divisions among them. The fact that there was no imminent threat to Israel's existence from Lebanon and that the Hezbollah guerrillas largely focused their operations against Israeli troops on Lebanese soil raised questions in the minds of the Israeli public about the need to stay in Lebanon and about justifying even the smallest number of Israeli casualties. Had Hezbollah framed its objectives in terms of eradicating Israel rather than liberating Lebanon, and had it sent suicide bombers to kill Israeli civilians, Israel's motivation would have been significantly different. At a minimum, motivation affects each side's threshold of pain and its will to exercise power. To achieve independence, Lebanon could endure immense pain; for no obvious vital interests, Israel could endure little. This issue of motivation is also affected by outside notions of the legitimacy of each side's cause: the sense that Lebanon's drive to seek independence was in harmony with the principles of sovereignty that most around the world accept generated more international sympathy for Lebanon than for Israel—which in turn reinforced the determination of the Lebanese.

The Palestinian-Israeli confrontation in the West Bank and Gaza has been of a different nature. Here too Israel has had overwhelming power superiority. The Palestinians had even more motivation than the Lebanese because they had no state at all and were under occupation. Their threshold of pain has thus been very high because the issue is ultimately about existence. For Israel, three issues made the question of motivation significantly different than the situation in Lebanon: First, the proximity of the West Bank to the heart of Israel makes the outcome much more important. Second, a significant portion of the Israeli population has always wanted to claim the West Bank as part of Israel. Third, the suicide bombings of civilians inside Israel have made the issue more vital because the threat is more immediate. As a consequence, even though the Palestinians have inflicted many more casualties on Israel than Hezbollah has, Israeli motivation has increased rather than diminished. Thus, the balance of motivation on the Israeli-Palestinian front fuels the conflict even more than the actual distribution of military power and reduces the chance that the conflict can be won through Palestinian attacks or through Israel's military superiority. Israel can inflict far more pain on the Palestinians than it suffers, but that is not the same as winning or achieving peace.

For a powerful America, it is important to keep in mind in contemplating military options globally, as in the Middle East, that motivation is a factor affecting the utility of power and the will to use it. Those who live in the Middle East will care more deeply about its future than we will. No strategy to defend American interests in areas such as Iraq and the rest of the Persian Gulf can succeed in the long run unless the United States ensures that it does not increase its deeply motivated enemies in the process.

3. The Nature of the Challenge and the Necessary Response

Understanding the Challenge

American power can fully address threats to vital U.S. interests emanating from any state or combination of states. As I argued in Chapter 1, terrorism is a threat that emanates largely from nonstate actors. It is not surprising that none of the terrorists who attacked America came from countries that our State Department labels "terrorist states," nor were they evidently connected to any such countries. Our military capabilities are sufficient to deter the most ambitious governments around the world, and every state, including Iran and North Korea, is sensitive to the deterrence of more powerful parties. U.S. military might is a primary reason why Saddam Hussein did not employ his chemical weapons in 1991, when our own military simulations showed that such an act would have resulted in thousands of American casualties. Deterrence worked: As former Secretary of State James Baker warned, the use of such weapons would have been the end of Saddam's government. However, it is much harder to deter motivated individuals and small groups that often thrive where central authority is weak and where deterrence is therefore less effective. In an era when states have less control over the flow of information and technology, it is increasingly easy for motivated groups and individuals who are willing to take risks to carry out terror attacks, and the threats they pose are likely to be increasingly lethal.

Certainly states can cooperate to minimize the threat, which ultimately is a threat to them all; the very logic of sovereignty in the international system is built on governments' monopoly of the use of force. But since the problem is global, it cannot be addressed unilaterally. The strategy can succeed only through significant cooperation with other states in intelligence, finance, and direct confrontation of threatening groups. A policy that brings about regional instability—through a spill-over of Iraqi instability and the inflammation of public opinion in the region—and with it a weakening of states on the one hand and a loss of their willful cooperation on the other, will fail to reduce the terrorist threat.

Consider, for example, the serious fear that terrorists may acquire weapons of mass destruction. In the past decade, the legitimate global concern was not that sovereign states would make such weapons available to terrorists but that the disintegration of the Soviet Union meant the loss of full control over these weapons in the former Soviet states. Even the reported discovery in 2002 that members of al-Qaeda or other groups were apparently experimenting with chemical weapons in northern Iraq was telling: Such experimentation didn't take place in areas where the Iraqi government had control but in the semiautonomous Kurdish areas that were

partly protected by U.S. air power. After the 2003 war, reports indicated that some terror groups were moving into
Iraq. Where there is less sovereignty, there is more chance
for terrorism.

Terrorism has a "demand side" as well as a "supply side,"
as I argued in Chapter 1. A military strategy could erode the
power of some of the suppliers, the organizations that tap
into popular disaffection to recruit members and plan attacks. But the demand side would remain: the public anger,
despair, and humiliation that motivate people to join such
groups. As long as that demand side remains or, even worse,
increases, the vacuum created by the destruction of one supplier will quickly be filled by other aspirants. Not all, or even
most, people who are desperate or feel a sense of deep humiliation are inclined to be recruited by groups engaged in
terror. But when one looks at a society as a whole and finds
that majorities are enraged, it is usually an indication that
people on the margins of that society are being radicalized
into sometimes brutal action.

Increasingly, public attitudes in the Arab world and much
of the Muslim world have included not only strong resentment of American foreign policy but also a sense of deep despair and humiliation that people connect in their minds to
that policy. Enhanced American dominance in the Gulf region is likely to add to that feeling. And despite the best of
intentions after 9/11, the debates in America and in the Arab
and Muslim worlds have increasingly portrayed the confrontation as involving America on the one hand and Arabs
and Muslims on the other. This phenomenon is dangerous

because it puts both sides on a slippery slope toward a long-term confrontation that benefits no one.

Although there are many issues accounting for the differences between the United States and many in the Arab and Muslim worlds, there is no escaping the fact that the Arab-Israeli conflict is the biggest source of anger and humiliation. Without this issue there would still be many differences, as there are between the United States and other parts of the world. But the depth of anger that motivates many people and creates ready recruits for terrorist organizers would be reduced. It would also become easier to work with regional actors to address common problems.

There can be no pretending that the structure of America's relationship with the Middle East is not centrally affected by the Arab-Israeli conflict; wars such as a new one with Iraq would only stun the region into a temporary lull before the reality reappears: America *is* a central player in the Arab-Israeli issue. The American commitment to Israel, which often pits the United States against all others in international organizations, means that when Israel is threatened, the United States must respond. On the other hand, when Israel prevails and Arabs are on the losing side, America will inevitably receive much of the blame for providing Israel with military, economic, and political support. The anger toward Israel increasingly becomes anger toward America as well. In the long term, no reordering of regional politics can resolve that dilemma except the resolution of the Arab-Israeli conflict, especially the Palestinian issue. Only peace between Israelis and Arabs can significantly reduce the challenge to

America's interests in the region. No other issue is as central to America's interest in the Middle East and to reducing the demand side of regional terrorism.

The Need to Build Bridges of Mutual Understanding

It is much easier to destroy bridges than to build them, but more bridges of understanding must be built between the United States and the people in Arab and Muslim countries. Invariably, public opinion surveys indicate that a primary source of Arab and Muslim frustration and anger toward the United States is a perceived lack of empathy for their pain and hardship. Even aside from the rights and wrongs of policy on issues such as Iraq and the Palestinian-Israeli conflict, the prevalent perception is that America does not value the lives of Arabs and Muslims. Effective public diplomacy is an essential component of American foreign policy in the region.

Public diplomacy is not the same as propaganda, and there are limits to what can be achieved through this means. The United States needs to explain its policies and to disseminate information about American culture, values, and aims. But public diplomacy must be present at the inception of any policy and must include dialogue and feedback: If the aim of policy is to send messages to others or to generate particular responses, it cannot succeed without understanding those others' aims, aspirations, priorities, and sensitivities.

Sometimes a single word from the president or secretary of state can outweigh millions of dollars spent on a campaign of public diplomacy. Two examples from recent history are telling. The first is President Bush's inadvertent use of the term *crusade* in describing the global campaign against terrorism because in the Muslim world that word evokes fears of a Christian crusade against Islam. It is as if the president of Egypt or Pakistan declared a new global policy aimed at America based on *jihad*, a term that is understood in the United States to mean Islamic holy war, though it is often used by Arabs and Muslims to mean simply struggle or campaign. Although the president later corrected the implication and began using different terms, his early statement continued to be used against him in the region as reflecting the true intent of U.S. policy.

A second example of words that were *not* said took place during the emotional period of destructive Israeli operations in Palestinian cities, ordered by Ariel Sharon after horrific suicide bombings that killed many Israeli civilians. Just as Israelis were understandably focused on their own pain and tragedy, Arabs were moved by the deaths of so many Palestinian civilians, the damage to their cities, and their helplessness in the face of a powerful Israeli army as displayed live on their television screens. These images reinforced their association of Sharon with war, violence, and a 1982 massacre of Palestinians in Lebanon. They waited to hear from the White House, hoping for plans to put an end to violence or at least words of empathy. However, President Bush described Sharon as a "man of peace." These words were posted over pictures of death and destruction in the Arab press and undermined everything else the president said.

There is another important reason for building bridges and establishing dialogue with people in the region in the campaign against terrorism in particular. As I have argued earlier in this book, terrorism is an immoral means employed by different groups for different ends. To reduce its occurrence, it must be delegitimized by societies where it occurs. To succeed, the war on terrorism must be seen not as an American war against specific groups but as a campaign to render the use of terrorist methods illegitimate, to make it harder for groups to recruit, to gain points, to be accepted. Such a policy would mean building a coalition and projecting moral consistency, for legitimacy and illegitimacy are ultimately about consensus and cannot be created alone. An effective policy must strive to prevent the perception that the conflict is between "us" and "them" in the sense of Americans versus Muslims and Arabs, constituting a clash of civilizations. It must recognize the internal struggle in the Arab and Muslim worlds for the fate of society, with significant, influential portions of these societies sharing many of our values, if not our policies. Empowering and helping those forces wage their own struggle for change is essential in winning the battle for hearts and minds.

Such empowerment cannot be addressed only through public diplomacy, which is about projecting information, images, and values to foreign publics. The ability of moderates to speak out in society—even in a free society—is limited in times of national crisis. When there is a sense of national pain, voices of dissent are often seen as unpatriotic, disloyal, or serving the interests of adversaries. Debate is muted, hard-liners play on public emotions, and moderates go on the defensive. It is an unfortunate phenomenon that appears everywhere, including in our own free country, but it is even more prevalent where society is less free. Although many in the Middle East reject the use of terrorism, few have spoken out as tension with the United States has grown over the Arab-Israeli issue. This silence is driven sometimes by self-censorship, sometimes by intimidation, and sometimes simply by anger: "If the United States cannot feel our pain, we will not feel its pain." Hence, American policy is very much a factor in affecting the prospects, shape, and outcome of such debates in the Middle East.

The role of governments and official policies in times of national crisis is essential for setting the tone of national debates and for helping mobilize moderates to confront those who support extreme options because they are blinded by fear or pain. Governments in the Middle East have a central role to play in the internal debate, and our own government has much influence in setting a tone of friendship and empathy that empowers and assists moderate forces. A policy that creates genuine peaceful alternatives is the best way to empower moderates, to rally them, to enable them to put forth a prospect of hope as they publicly debate the voices of militancy. Such policy alternatives need not always originate in Washington, as the United States must find ways to work with others in the region and elsewhere. American backing for efforts of the European Union, or for ideas such as the Saudi peace proposals, could be used to enhance American interests as well as the prospects of peace in the Middle East.

4. The Values at Stake

I have argued that a compassionate approach, one that builds coalitions and considers the vital interests of other states, one that does not disregard the wishes of people around the globe, is also a prudent approach generally, and certainly toward the Middle East. It is as essential for a successful foreign policy as the measured exercise of power itself. But compassion is also an end in itself—especially for those powerful enough to afford it. I began this book by expressing the fears in reaction to the horror that befell our nation: a fear of the actual threat posed by terrorism in today's world, and the worry that our response to that fear will undermine the very values that make our nation great.

America's success in contemporary politics has certainly been bolstered by its superior military power. But that military power itself is a product of a successful economic and political system that reflects what America stands for. Those around the world who have sought change of their own political and economic systems have done so in large part on their own and not because America forced its ideas on them. Success is a model. Those who want to match it will have to emulate the model, and those who don't will likely fail. Powerful ideas are intentionally accepted or rejected by those who compete in the global market; ideas win by inspiring, not by threatening. Democracy is part of the success story of America. Even those who are reluctant to embrace it, such as Chinese leaders, have understood the need to emulate much of America's economic approach lest they be left further behind. In embracing a new economic approach, such nations have also unleashed a political process they will not be able to fully control.

Some believe that we can spread democracy through war, but it should be apparent that democracy is about the will of the people, about their right to choose. Ultimately, our role in that issue is to cooperate, to assist, and above all to inspire. Democracy, by definition, cannot be imposed. The thought that because we have the power, we should disregard the wishes of other people around the globe on issues that are often more vital to them than to us—and that we know what's best for others better than they do themselves—would not be comforting to most Americans.

No other society has been as open, egalitarian, diverse, or hospitable to immigrants as America's. This openness is part of America's greatness and its political and economic success. A policy toward the Arab and Muslim worlds that has the effect of turning America into a fortress, building barriers between the United States and nations that comprise over a billion people, and allowing fear to compromise civil liberties even in our own land is not the stuff of greatness. We may succeed tactically in the short term but only by losing ourselves, what we stand for. In the end, we become what we do.

Epilogue

This book was originally written after the tragedy of 9/11, 2001, and before the Iraq war in the spring of 2003. Since then, many of the fears held by skeptics of the Iraq war plan, including concerns that I had expressed in earlier chapters of this book, deepened as the consequences of the war unfolded.

On the eve of the war, in early March 2003 and in conjunction with Zogby International, I conducted a survey in six Arab countries (Egypt, Saudi Arabia, Morocco, Lebanon, Jordan, and the United Arab Emirates) and the United States.[1] Not surprisingly, the vast majority of Arabs opposed the war. Other surveys, including one by Pew in Muslim countries, revealed similar levels of opposition, largely (and disturbingly) for reasons relating to a deep mistrust of America's intentions. In every country we surveyed, most of the respondents suggested that the primary objectives of the United States were to secure oil and to help Israel—not to spread democracy, fight terrorism, eliminate weapons of mass destruction, or advance Middle East peace.

In the months after the war, these regional suspicions of American foreign policy were reinforced. No serious evidence materialized to link the Iraqi regime with al-Qaeda, despite the repeated assertions of the American government prior to the war. In addition, the inability to discover weapons of mass destruction (WMD), and the fact that Saddam Hussein's regime did not employ such weapons during the war, have also deepened the fear that the primary stated explanation for the war, WMD, was a mere rationalization for other American objectives. Many Arab governments, facing strong internal opposition to the war but having, in effect, supported the U.S. effort, were inclined to bridge the gap between their public sentiment and their own actions by becoming even less democratic. Indeed, the government of the one Muslim democracy in the Middle East, Turkey, was forced to respond to its public opinion by forgoing more than $10 billion in American aid and reversing an understanding to allow American forces to wage war from Turkish soil, even as these forces waited in ships off Turkey's shores.

In Iraq, it was clear that the hatred for Saddam Hussein's regime, even among the Shiite population in the south, did not translate into an acceptance of the American presence. The continuing divisions within Iraq complicated the emergence of an effective government. The vital interests of neighboring states such as Iran, Turkey, and Syria, were major complicating factors in bringing stability to Iraq. Given the destruction of most social and political organizations by the Saddam Hussein regime, the best-organized remaining groups were the religious organizations, raising fears in the United States about the possibility of a clergy regime, perhaps similar to Iran's, if early elections were held.

It became clear that any stable outcome in Iraq would take time to materialize, even under the best of circumstances. In the short term, the near anarchy in parts of Iraq led to visible suffering: the absence of personal security; the lack of the most basic essential services, such as water and electricity; and the rise of such painful phenomena as kidnapping and prostitution. All this, which received much coverage in the Arab press, prevented the projection of Iraq as a model to be followed in the Arab world. It played instead into the hands of authoritarian regimes who resist change by overwhelming with negative perceptions and realities the positive possibilities that might otherwise have resulted from the demise of the ruthless regime of Saddam Hussein.

On the Arab-Israeli issue, which remains the prism through which most Arabs evaluate American actions, early hope for the revival of the prospects for peace between Israel and the Palestinians gave way to despair by early fall of 2003. To be sure, the Bush Administration, in conjunction with the Russians, the European Union, and the UN (the so-called Quartet), put forth a peace plan (the "Road Map") that seemed promising in the early weeks following the Iraq war.[2] But the Road Map had originally been prepared prior to the Iraq war, in part to alleviate fears that the United States was pursuing war at the expense of Arab-Israeli peace. It was thus more a set of ideas than a self-implementing plan. It contained many contradictions that prevented its implementation.

Certainly, events on the ground—continued terrorist attacks against Israeli civilians, nonstop construction of Israeli settlements in the occupied West Bank, and the building of a wall-and-fence structure[3] by Israel—made matters worse. But the problems were even more profound than was acknowledged by those who simply blamed matters on the flaws of Palestinian leader Yasser Arafat or Israeli Prime Minister Ariel Sharon.

The plan assumed that Israeli and Palestinian leaders truly accepted its propositions. Yet, there is much evidence that this was not the case. It is hard to know what Yasser Arafat intended, but it is easier to know that Mr. Sharon did not envision a full final settlement that would be minimally acceptable to the Palestinians within the three-year timetable suggested by the plan. In responding to the plan, both Israelis and Palestinians were mostly responding to the U.S. demand, not to each other, trying to minimize the degree of American opposition and to attract maximum American support. This meant that for the plan to work, the United States would have to elevate Arab–Israeli peacemaking to the top of its priorities and to expend political leverage at home and abroad.

If the hope before the war was that the President's leverage at home and abroad would be so enhanced as to ensure the success of the American peace efforts, the consequences did not match the expectations. First, Iraq became an even higher priority for the United States than before, as about

150,000 American troops remained on Iraqi soil facing what increasingly looked like guerrilla warfare, costing about $4 billion every month. This of course, was in addition to the continuing war on terrorism, especially in Afghanistan. In this regard, Arab-Israeli peacemaking was bound to be a lesser priority. Second, increasing questions about the war in the United States lessened the President's popularity by the fall of 2003 and thus diminished his domestic leverage. Third, the beginning of the American Presidential campaign, and the inevitable focus on important domestic issues, especially the economy, were bound to take precedent. In the end, the Road Map would be left at the mercy of the local actors whose mistrust of each other reached a low point.

Here was the problem: In the midst of the daily pain of occupation and violence, and progressively diminishing trust, each party was being asked to make concessions at every step that entailed giving up leverage for the more important next step. This formula could not succeed in any negotiations, even were the parties to negotiate in good faith. In this environment, and given the minimal American involvement, each side had to assume that the prospects of failure were greater than the prospects of success. Given this calculation, each side was bound to act in preparation for failure instead of maximizing the chance of success. This was a sure prescription for unilateralism and failure.

Likely as it is to continue, the Israeli-Palestinian conflict will remain the biggest obstacle to an effective American policy in the Middle East. This time, it will come in the shadow of changed relationships between the United States and the governments in the region following the Iraq war. In this regard, it is fair to say that while the public in the Arab world became even more resentful of the United States, some governments in the region worried about their own fate immediately after the Iraq war. Certainly the early sense that American power had once again succeeded in toppling an entrenched regime with ease, and the demonstration that the United States was willing and able to go it alone, did propel some governments in the region to anxious concern.

But such concern did not last long. For it became clear that what appeared to be an early success did not warrant celebration, as the struggle for Iraq began to look like it could take years, with a successful outcome by no means assured. On the one hand, the United States could not afford to lose the after-war struggle in Iraq. Otherwise, enemies of America, especially militant groups, might be emboldened to resist America's power of deterrence. On the other hand, America's success depended on tying up its military, financial, and diplomatic resources for an extended period of time, significantly stretching if not overcommitting American might. It became obvious to many that America's ability to engage in another war with states like Iran or North Korea was certainly diminished, not enhanced—at least in the foreseeable future.

Strategically, what I had anticipated in the earlier chapters of this book before the war seemed to take shape in a manner disturbing to American interests. The expected acceleration of nuclear programs by states who may have feared they could become the next targets of United States intervention apparently materialized in the case of both North Korea, which had declared the development of nuclear weapons, and Iran, which aroused increased suspicions that it may be trying to follow the same path. At the same time, given the suspicions that have been raised about the U.S. case for Iraqi weapons of mass destruction, fewer around the world and at home were likely to accept American assertions about the possible nuclear capabilities of states like Iran.

The global concern about American unilateralism has propelled the emergence of counter-coalitions at the UN, especially by Russia, Germany, and France, often supported by China. It has become clear since the Iraq war that these states are much more willing to take on the United States in international organizations and that they are much less willing to send their own troops and resources to Iraq. To be sure, the United States still has leverage, both because of its overwhelming military power in the region and, most importantly, because even states like France, who were fearful that a quick American success in Iraq might embolden Washington to follow suit elsewhere, were almost equally terrified by the prospect of American failure in Iraq. Many European and Middle East governments alike fear militant Islamist groups; their opposition to American foreign policy was primarily about means, not ends. There was a sense that if America were to fail in Iraq because of continued militant attacks, the consequence would embolden and increase the power of the very groups that even many of America's critics fear.

In all the discussion about Iraq, it was seemingly forgotten that the war was justified in the minds of the American public because of the understandable fear of terrorism after the horror of 9/11. While it is clear that there was no evidence linking Saddam Hussein and his government to 9/11, and some evidence to the contrary, opinion surveys in the United States in the summer of 2003 showed that about 70 percent of Americans believed that such connections existed. A survey by PIPA in September 2003 suggested a possible link between this belief and the degree of public support for the war.[4] Regardless of the role that our government and media played in helping to develop such impressions (in contrast, for example, to polls immediately after 9/11 that showed that few Americans believed Saddam Hussein was involved[5]), proponents of the war certainly argued that the toppling of the Iraq regime would reduce terrorism. This notion that sees terrorism primarily as a tool of states, as discussed in the first chapter in this book, has been challenged by the events following the war. The anarchy in Iraq has not only led to the proliferation of militant groups within Iraq, but may have created an environment hospitable to the hosting of external terrorist groups, including possibly al-Qaeda—groups that had not been known to exist in Iraq before. Such breeding of terrorist groups is a troubling and unintended, if predictable, outcome of instability.

In the end, the ultimate success of American foreign policy in the Middle East and around the globe will depend on the success of the United States in bringing about a stable, prosperous, and reasonably democratic Iraq, and on the fate of Arab–Israeli peace. The outcome is by no means clear. But the challenges may now be even greater than they were before the Iraq war, and certainly greater than they were before the tragedy of 9/11.

The most dangerous trend is an increasing perception in Muslim countries that the United States is specifically targeting and weakening Muslims, matched by the heightened fears of many Americans about Muslim aims toward America and the West. A good picture comes from Turkey, a strong ally of the United States since World War II, a Muslim country with a more democratic system than most countries in the region, and a system perceived by American policymakers as a model for moderation and democracy in the Muslim world, especially after 9/11.

Like other Muslims around the world, the vast majority of Turks opposed the Iraq war. But what was most disturbing was that much of their opposition was based on the sense that the United States was targeting a Muslim country. The issue of Islamic identity was thus elevated in the Turkish relationship with the United States even above, for example, Turkish national interests on such matters as the fear of a breakaway Kurdish state (under the impetus of an alliance between separatist Turkish Kurds with suddenly liberated Kurds in Iraq). This dangerous tone was brought home by a frightening image I encountered in Istanbul, Turkey, in the summer of 2003, while on a mission of a congressionally mandated Advisory Group, appointed by the Bush Administration and empowered to examine American public diplomacy toward the Arab and Muslim world. A grand old building in the center of the city, across a narrow street from offices and apartments where many of the city's people mingled, once housed a vibrant American Consulate accessible to a friendly population. Now, however, a few miles away, on the outskirts of Istanbul, on a commanding hill, surrounded by walls and much security, sits an enormous, lonely, fortresslike structure that houses the new American consulate. As I stood in a tower on the edge of the structure, looking far down into a middle-class Turkish neighborhood, I had the chilling sense that Turks below were seeing a Crusader castle.

It should be evident from what I have argued in this book that a clash of civilizations between the United States and the Muslim and Arab world is by no means a natural outcome—and certainly not an inevitable one. For one thing, "the Muslim and Arab world" is very diverse, with many states who often have more in conflict with each other than with the United States. But there is a danger that we may be on a slippery slope that can take us toward that mutually devastating end if both the United States and the governments in the region do not work to reverse the clashing courses. The stakes are high for the United States and for the Middle East.

NOTES

Chapter 1

1. U.S. Department of State, 2000 "Patterns of Global Terrorism" report, released April 2001 by the secretary of state and the coordinator for counterterrorism (http://www.state.gov/s/ct/rls/pgtrtp/2000)

2. Velupillai Prabakaran, chief of the Liberation Tigers of Tamil Eelam, Heroes' Day speech, November 27, 2001 (Available at: http://www.eelamweb.com/leader/messages/herosday/2001/english/

Chapter 2

1. Council on Foreign Relations Independent Task Force report, *Public Diplomacy: A Strategy for Reform* (New York: CFR Press, July 2002).

2. Poll published in the *International Herald Tribune*, August 15, 2001. Survey conducted by the Pew Research Center in partnership with the *International Herald Tribune* and in association with the Council on Foreign Relations.

3. The 2002 Gallup Poll of the Islamic World. Ten thousand people in nine predominantly Islamic countries were interviewed. In December 2001 and January 2002, researchers conducted hour-long, in-person interviews in Saudi Arabia, Iran, Pakistan, Indonesia, Turkey, Lebanon, Kuwait, Jordan, and Morocco.

4. Henrique Cardoso's speech—from "Anti-Americanism in Brazil" by Kenneth Maxwell, published in *Correspondence: An International Review of Culture and Society*, No. 9, Spring, 2002. Copyright 2002 by the Council on Foreign Relations, Inc. All rights reserved. (Found on website – http://www.brazilnetwork.org/analysis1.htm). Former South African President Nelson Mandela called the American unilateral approach "a threat to

world peace." (From *Newsweek* online. Interview by Tom Masland "Nelson Mandela: The USA Is a Threat to World Peace." September 10, 2002).

5. Gallup International poll on terrorism, a sixty-country survey conducted in November and December 2001 by members of Gallup International Association (GIA) around the world.

6. Zogby International, "The Ten-Nation Impressions of America" poll, face-to-face interviews in Egypt, France, Indonesia, Iran, Kuwait, Lebanon, Pakistan, Saudi Arabia, the United Arab Emirates, and Venezuela between March 4 and April 3, 2002. Released April 11, 2002.

7. Program on International Policy Attitudes (PIPA) poll, "Americans on the Arab-Israeli Conflict." PIPA is a joint program of the Center on Policy Attitudes (COPA) and the Center for International and Security Studies at Maryland (CISSM), School of Public Affairs, University of Maryland. PIPA conducted an in-depth study of American public attitudes on the Israeli-Palestinian conflict by reviewing existing polling from other organizations, conducting focus groups in Chicago and Baltimore, and conducting a nationwide poll of 802 randomly selected Americans on May 1–5, 2002 (margin of error plus or minus 3.5–4 percent).

8. Committee on Foreign Affairs Hearings: Post-War Policy Issues in the Persian Gulf (1991), 102d Congress, 1st sess., 120. Washington, D.C.: U.S. Government Printing Office.

9. The 2002 Gallup Poll of the Islamic World (see note 3).

10. The 2002 Gallup Poll of the Islamic World.

11. Reports in Kuwaiti papers reprinted by Federal Bureau of Information Services (FBIS), *FBIS Daily Report*, June 25, 1990 (FBIS-NES–90–122).

12. Egyptian President Hosni Mubarak, quoted in *FBIS Daily Report*, June 5, 1990 (FBIS-NES–90–108).

13. Founded in 1951, America-Mideast Educational and Training Services, Inc. (AMIDEAST) is a private, nonprofit organization working to strengthen mutual understanding and cooperation between Americans and the people of the Middle East and North Africa. Headquartered in Washington, D.C., AMIDEAST maintains a network of field offices in Egypt, Jordan, Kuwait, Lebanon, Morocco, Syria, Tunisia, the United Arab Emirates, the West Bank/Gaza Strip, and Yemen.

14. Lyndon H. Larouche, Jr., "Zbigniew Brzezinski and September 11th," *Executive Intelligence Review* 29, 1 (January 11, 2002).

Chapter 3

1. Jimmy Carter, *Keeping Faith* (Toronto, New York, London, Sydney: Bantam Books, 1982), p. 358.

2. From U.S. Senate Committee on Foreign Relations Hearing on Iraq (transcribed from C-SPAN broadcast), July 31, 2002.

3. Ross appeared on the al-Jazeera talk show *Al Ittijah Al Mo'akis* on November 20, 2001 (following the bombing of al-Jazeera's bureau in Afghanistan on November 13, 2001).

4. Mohammad Affash Adwan, information minister of Jordan, Wednesday, August 8, 2002, in response to a program titled "Opposite Direction" broadcast by al-Jazeera on Tuesday, August 6, 2002, in which Assad Abu-Khalil, a professor at a U.S. university, appeared.

5. Thomas L. Friedman, *The Lexus and the Olive Tree* (New York: Farrar, Straus, and Giroux, 1999), p. 12.

6. Henry Kissinger, *Years of Upheaval* (Boston: Little, Brown, 1982), p. 465.

Chapter 4

1. Saddam Hussein, speech on August 8, 2002, on the occasion of the fourteenth anniversary of the 1980–1988 Iraq-Iran war. The text of the Saddam Hussein speech is on BBC Radio 4 at http://www.bbc.co.uk/ radio4/today/reports/international/saddam_speech.shtml

2. Zogby International, "The Ten-Nation Impressions of America" poll, face-to-face interviews in Egypt, France, Indonesia, Iran, Kuwait, Lebanon, Pakistan, Saudi Arabia, the United Arab Emirates, and Venezuela between March 4 and April 3, 2002. Released April 11, 2002.

3. Shibley Telhami, "If at First You Don't Succeed Postpone," *Los Angeles Times*, July 14, 2000, B9.

4. Shibley Telhami, "Avoiding Blame in Mideast Summit," *Baltimore Sun*, July 27, 2000.

5. Report of the Sharm el-Sheikh Fact-Finding Committee (also known as "The Mitchell Report"), April 30, 2001.

6. Joshua S. Goldstein, Jon C. Pevehouse, Deborah J. Gerner, and Shibley Telhami, "Reciprocity, Triangularity, and Cooperation in the Middle East, 1979–97," *Journal of Conflict Resolution* 45, 5 (October 2001): 594–620.

Chapter 5

1. Shibley Telhami, *Power and Leadership in International Bargaining: The Path to the Camp David Accords* (New York: Columbia University Press, 1990), p. 73.

2. Shibley Telhami, "The Persian Gulf: Understanding the American Oil Strategy," *The Brookings Review* 20, 2 (Spring 2002): 32–35.

Epilogue

1. For details and discussion of the survey, see "Arab Public Opinion—A Survey in Six Countries," by Shibley Telhami, *San Jose Mercury News*, Sunday, March 16, 2003, and "Arab Public Opinion of the United States and Iraq" by Shibley Telhami, *Brookings Review* 21, 3 (Summer 2003) 24–27.

2. The Road Map, most of which was developed before the war, was released by the State department on April 30th, 2003. Designed to propose steps toward the establishment of a viable, contiguous Palestinian state at peace with Israel within three years, it called for an end to terrorism, a freeze in the construction and growth of Jewish settlements in the West Bank and Gaza, Palestinian reform measures, among other steps, within three short phases. Phase I was termed "Ending Terror And Violence, Normalizing Palestinian Life, and Building Palestinian Institutions;" Phase II was termed "Transition;" and the final stage was the "Permanent Status Agreement and End of the Israeli-Palestinian Conflict."

3. The barrier was built inside the West Bank. About 90 miles of construction was completed by fall 2003, and the overall length could eventually total 400 miles. The barrier is from 60–100 yards wide, and could extend more than 15 miles into the West Bank. It is made up, among other things, of barbed wire, electronic sensors, concrete walls, trenches, razor wire, roads, cameras, guard towers, and steel fences. Certain parts of the fence would have gaps and be patrolled by troops. Israel said it was building it for security, while critics argued that its location (not on the 1967 borders but inside the West Bank) disrupted Palestinian life and that, like settlements, it sent a signal that Israel was intending to annex parts of West Bank, thus eroding Palestinian confidence in the negotiations. The Bush Administration expressed its concern about the barrier.

4. The poll was conducted by the Program on International Policy Attitudes (PIPA) at the University of Maryland and Knowledge Networks, released October 2, 2003. It found wide misperceptions on Iraq highly related to support for war. The report can be found at this link: http://www.pipa.org/OnlineReports/Iraq/Media_10_02_03_Report.pdf

5. The poll was conducted by Wirthlin Worldwide, September 15–17, 2001. When asked "Who do you think is more responsible for the recent terrorist attacks on the New York World Trade Center and the Pentagon?" only 3 percent proposed Saddam Hussein or Iraq as the most likely suspect. Cited by Program on International Policy Analysis. For reference, please go to their link: http://www.americans-world.org/digest/regional_issues/Conflict_Iraq/linkstoTerr.cfm

INDEX

199

DISCUSSION QUESTIONS

On Terrorism and the Role of Religion

- The author makes the argument that terrorism has both a "supply side" and a "demand side." What does he mean? What is the demand side of terrorism and what are the factors that affect it? Can a policy aimed at reducing the occurrence of terrorism succeed without addressing both the demand side and the supply side of terrorism?

- *The Stakes* suggests that terrorism is not an ideology like communism, or a movement that can be defeated simply by targeting a particular group. Do you agree with that? What is terrorism? Is it merely an instrument used by different groups for different ends or is it a political coalition that could be directly confronted? Can the effort to confront terrorism be merely military or are there other components to a successful strategy? What role do moral notions play in the struggle?

- The author suggests that the greatest threat emanating from groups like al-Qaeda is the fact that they are nonstate actors. What is the basis of this argument? What is the role of states in the terrorist phenomenon? Is it easier to deter states or nonstate actors? Why?

- Do terrorist groups thrive in highly centralized and stable states or in unstable environments where state control is weak? What are the implications of your conclusions for desirable policies intended to reduce the threat of terrorism?

- Since the tragedy of 9/11, the focus, understandably, has been on terrorism emanating from the Middle East specifically. Is terrorism a Middle Eastern phenomenon or is it a global phenomenon? What are the global terrorist trends? Has the Middle East led the world in terrorism in the past decade? What explains suicide terrorism? Is it limited to religious groups? to Islamic groups? to the Middle East?

- In recent years, much of the terrorism emanating from the Middle East has been conducted in the name of Islam. What explains this trend? Have religious groups always been associated with terrorism and violence in the Middle East? If not, what explains the changing trends? What are the policy implications of your conclusions?

Sources of Resentment of American Foreign Policy

- After the 9/11 tragedy many Americans asked "Why do they hate us so much?" Does this question apply equally to al-Qaeda and to the general public in Arab and Muslim countries? Is there a difference between the two? Do people in the Middle East really "hate" America?

- Have Arabs and Muslims always resented the United States? What are the historical trends in public attitudes toward the United States? How do these compare with attitudes toward European nations? What do these trends tell you about the sources of resentment?

- In addressing the sources of Arab resentment toward the United States, the author suggests putting the issue in "global context." What does he mean? Are there similar trends in other parts of the world? What are the implications of your conclusion? In what ways are Arab attitudes similar to the attitudes of others and in what ways are they different?

- What are the sources of resentment toward the United States in the Arab world? Do Arabs resent American values or do they resent American policies? Does this make a difference? What does the evidence suggest? Which are the important policy issues for most people in the region?

The Role of Public Opinion and the Media

- American foreign policy has often ignored public opinion in the Middle East on the basis of the following proposition: Most governments in the region are authoritarian and can dictate, influence, or ignore the public in making decisions. Thus, it is best to focus American policy on influencing governments, not public opinion. What do you think of this approach? What are its limits?

- Is public opinion in the Middle East irrelevant? Do governments in the region have to be concerned about their public opinion? Why? What are the implications if governments continue to ignore their public attitudes?

- Can governments today fully shape public opinion in the Middle East? Were they able to do so in the past? What has changed in recent years that makes it increasingly hard for governments to spin news to their liking?

- What is distinctive about the "new media" in the Middle East, especially satellite television? Who is their audience? How broad is their reach? What is their relationship with governments?

- What are the benefits of the information revolution for the region? What are the risks and the dangers? Overall, are the benefits of such television stations as *al-Jazeera* more positive or more negative for the region or for US foreign policy?

- As we focus on the need for Arab countries to democratize, what are the implications of ignoring public opinion in the formation of our foreign policy? How might we address the need for reform while at the same time having to work with authoritarian governments?

The Role of the Arab-Israeli Issue

- In the debate about the sources of Arab anger with US foreign policy, the importance of the Arab-Israeli issue, especially the Palestinian-Israeli conflict, has been central. What is the evidence about the relative role of this issue in Arab attitudes toward the United States?
- It can be argued that many governments in the region have used the Palestinian-Israeli issue to divert attention from other domestic issues for which they don't want to be accountable. Does this mean that the issue is not central in the minds of the public? Does it mean the opposite?
- The author makes the case that the Palestinian-Israeli issue is one of "identity" for most Arabs. What is meant by this proposition? What is the evidence? Do you agree or disagree? What are the historical events that may have affected the relative importance of this issue in the minds of the public in the region? What recent events may have intensified the feelings?
- If you believe that the Arab-Israeli issue is central in the priorities of Arabs, what are the implications for the prospects of peace and stability in the region? What are the implications for US policy toward other issues in the region such as Iraq, oil, and democracy? Can these issues be fully separated?
- What was the basic notion leading to increased prospects of Palestinian-Israeli peace in the 1990s? What is the role of nationalism and mutual acceptance? How did each side interpret the collapse of negotiations in July 2000 and the subsequent advent of the *intifada*, the Palestinian uprising?
- What are the risks of sustained conflict? Do they increase or decrease the chance of eventual agreement? As each side suffers

increased losses, is it more or less likely to "give up"? Why? In your view, what is required for a breakthrough in the conflict?

The Role of the Persian Gulf Region

- The Persian Gulf region has been central in American foreign policy toward the Middle East for more than a half century, largely because of oil. Why is the region's oil so important to the United States and the rest of the world. Is it likely to become more or less important in the next decade? What are the trends?

- Why is Saudi Arabia so central on matters related to oil? What are the concerns about Saudi Arabia's political and economic system and their implications for the oil supply? What are the dangers and the opportunities today for Saudi reform? Can reform be imposed from the outside? If not, what's the alternative?

- What have been American calculations toward the oil region during the Cold War? What is "oil denial" strategy and how did it affect American strategy in the Middle East? How did this strategy evolve over time? Was the American fear based on a threat to the supply of oil to the West or on the possibility that enemy states might become more powerful if they came to control the oil supply?

- Besides the perceived Soviet threat to the region, were there other states or regimes whose power was feared by US foreign policy. What role have Iran and Iraq played in the region in the past several decades, and how did the United States address perceived threats emanating from both? What were the primary American fears after the Iraqi invasion of Kuwait in 1990?

- When polled, most people in the Arab world, and many others around the globe, believe that the US-led war to depose the government of Saddam Hussein was primarily over oil. Do you agree or disagree? How has the war affected the oil issue, if at all? What are the dangers and the opportunities that have emerged in Iraq after the war?

The Use of Force and its Limits

- Today the United States is the world's sole superpower, the mightiest of all nations. The ease with which the United States has disposed of two regimes in Afghanistan and Iraq has made everyone take notice. Can the United States pursue an effective foreign policy that relies primarily on the use of its extraordinary power?

- The author makes the point that power, no matter how superior, remains limited and can easily be depleted, that it is more effective the less it is used. Do you agree or disagree? In what ways is the United States stronger and what ways is it weaker after the war in Iraq?

- How effective is conventional power against states and how effective is it against nonstate actors? Can its deployment against states sometimes work in favor of nonstate actors, including terrorist groups? Has the war against Iraq brought more or less stability in the region? Has it increased or decreased the ability of terrorist groups to use Iraqi territory? In what ways has the war weakened groups like al-Qaeda? In what ways has it strengthened them?

- It is sometimes argued that an inequality of power between groups or states can be offset by the superior motivation of the seemingly weaker party. What is meant by this proposition? How do you assess the importance of motivation? What explains the fact that some parties are more motivated than others? What are the implications of this view for foreign policy?

- How important is it that the United States try to win the "hearts of minds" of people in the Middle East and around the world at the same time that it continues to fight al-Qaeda? What are the sorts of things the United States can do to win hearts and minds?

- Should the United States worry about the implications of its foreign policy abroad for what happens inside America itself? Some believe that the absence of clear international norms means that we are not bound by our own domestic standards when we act abroad. Do you agree with this notion? Are there risks that you see? Can what we do abroad be completely separated from who we are at home?

Selected Readings

For background on the origins of the twentieth-century system in the Middle East, see David Fromkin, *A Peace to End All Peace: The Fall of the Ottoman Empire and the Creation of the Modern Middle East* (Owl Books, 2001). For a useful book on US policy toward terrorism, see Paul Pillar, *Terrorism and US Foreign Policy* (Brookings, 2004). For a helpful introduction to Islam, see Karen Armstrong, *Islam: A Short History* (Random House, 2000). For two divergent interpretations of the role of Islam in politics, see John Esposito, *Unholy War: Terror in the Name of Islam* (Oxford University Press, 2002), and Bernard Lewis, *What Went Wrong: Western Impact and Middle Eastern Response* (Oxford University Press, 2001).

A good background on the Palestinian-Israeli conflict is provided by Mark A. Tessler, *A History of the Israeli-Palestinian Conflict* (Indiana University Press, 1994). For an excellent account of the US role in the conflict, see William B. Quandt, *Peace Process: American Diplomacy and the Arab-Israeli Conflict since 1967* (Revised Edition, University of California Press, co-published with Brookings Institution Press, 2001). An analysis of the failure of the negotiations is articulated by Charles Enderlin, *Shattered Dreams: The Failure of the Peace Process in the Middle East, 1995–2002* (Other Press, 2003).

An informative examination of Arab attitudes toward the United States, based on opinion surveys, is provided by Jim Zogby, *What*

Arabs Think: Values, Beliefs, and Concerns (Zogby International, 2002). For a collection of articles on the foreign policies of Middle Eastern states, see Shibley Telhami and Michael Barnett, eds., *Identity and Foreign Policy in the Middle East* (Cornell University Press, 2002). Four helpful books on the Arab media are Jon B. Alterman, *New Media, New Politics? From Satellite Television to the Internet in the Arab World* (Policy Paper No. 48, The Washington Institute for Near East Policy, 1998); Naomi Sakr, *Satellite Realms: Transnational Television, Globalization and the Middle East* (London and New York: I.B. Tauris, 2001); William Rugh, *Arab Mass Media: Newspapers, Radio, and Television in Arab Politics* (Praeger, 2004); and Mohammed El-Nawawy and Adel Iskandar, *Al-Jazeera: How the Free Arab News Network Scooped the World and Changed the Middle East* (Westview Press, 2002).

For a history of Iraq, see Phebe Marr, *The Modern History of Iraq*, Second Edition (Westview Press, 2003). For a general overview of trends in Middle East development, see Clement M. Henry and Robert Springborg, *Globalization and the Politics of Development in the Middle East* (Cambridge University Press, 2001). A good discussion of the limitations of American power is provided by Joseph Nye, *The Paradox of American Power: Why the World's Only Superpower Can't Go It Alone* (Oxford University Press, 2003). For the role of ethics and religion in American foreign policy, see Bryan Hehir, Michael Walzer, Charles Krauthammer, Louise Richardson, and Shibley Telhami, *Liberty and Power: A Dialogue on Religion and American Foreign Policy in an Unjust World* (Brookings, 2004).